# SHORT WALKS
# WYE VALLEY

by Mike Dunn

Brobury Scar below Monnington Walk (Walk 8)

# CONTENTS

# USING THIS GUIDE

## Routes in this book

In this book you will find a selection of easy or moderate walks suitable for almost everyone, including casual walkers and families with children, or for when you only have a short time to fill. The routes have been carefully chosen to allow you to explore the area and its attractions. Most routes are circular or out-and-back, although some linear walks may be included that use public transport to get back to the start. Although there may be some climbs there is no challenging terrain, but do bear in mind that conditions can sometimes be wet or muddy underfoot. A route summary table is included on page 6 to help you choose the right walk.

## Clothing and footwear

You won't need any special equipment to enjoy these walks. The weather in Britain can be changeable, so choose clothing suitable for the season and wear or carry a waterproof jacket. For footwear, comfortable walking boots or trainers with a good grip are best. A small rucksack for drinks, snacks and spare clothing is useful. See adventuresmart.uk.

## Walk descriptions

At the beginning of each walk you'll find all the information you need:

- start/finish location, with a what3words address to help you find it
- parking and transport information, estimated walking time, total distance and climb
- details of public toilets available along the route and where you can get refreshments
- a summary of the key highlights of the walk and what you might see

Timings given are the time to complete the walk at a reasonable walking pace. Allow extra time for extended stops or if walking with children.

The route is described in clear, easy-to-follow directions, with each waypoint marked on an accompanying map extract. It's a good idea to read the whole of the route instructions before setting out, so that you know what to expect.

## Maps, GPX files and what3words

Extracts from the OS® 1:25,000 map accompany each route. GPX files for all the walks in this book are available to download at cicerone.co.uk/1289/gpx.

What3words is a free smartphone app which identifies every 3m square of the globe with a unique three-word address, e.g. ///destiny.cafe.sonic. For more information see what3words.com/products/what3words-app.

## Walking with children

Even young children can be surprisingly strong walkers, but every family is different and you may need to adapt the timings given in this book to take that into account. Make sure you go at the pace of the slowest member and choose a walk with an exciting objective in mind, such as a cave, river, waterfall or picnic spot. Many of the walks can be shortened to suit – suggestions are included at the end of the route description.

## Dogs

Sheep or cattle may be found grazing on a number of these walks. Keep dogs under control at all times so that they don't scare or disturb livestock or wildlife. Cattle, particularly cows with calves, may very occasionally pose a risk to walkers with dogs. If you ever feel threatened by cattle, you should let go of your dog's lead and let it run free.

## Enjoying the countryside responsibly

Enjoy the countryside and treat it with respect to protect our natural environments. Stick to footpaths and take your litter home with you. When driving, slow down on rural roads and park considerately, or better still use public transport. For more details check out gov.uk/countryside-code.

### The Countryside Code

#### Respect everyone
- be considerate to those living in, working in and enjoying the countryside
- leave gates and property as you find them
- do not block access to gateways or driveways when parking
- be nice, say hello, share the space
- follow local signs and keep to marked paths unless wider access is available

#### Protect the environment
- take your litter home – leave no trace of your visit
- do not light fires and only have BBQs where signs say you can
- always keep dogs under control and in sight
- dog poo – bag it and bin it – any public waste bin will do
- care for nature – do not cause damage or disturbance

#### Enjoy the outdoors
- check your route and local conditions
- plan your adventure – know what to expect and what you can do
- enjoy your visit, have fun, make a memory

# ROUTE SUMMARY TABLE

| WALK NAME | START POINT | TIME | DISTANCE |
|---|---|---|---|
| 1. Chase Wood from Ross-on-Wye | Fernbank Road, Ross-on-Wye | 1hr 30min | 4.2km (2.6 miles) |
| 2. Ross-on-Wye and Wilton | Market House, Ross-on-Wye | 2hr | 5.8km (3.6 miles) |
| 3. Sellack Boat and Hoarwithy | King's Caple church | 2hr 45min | 8.2km (5.1 miles) |
| 4. Capler Camp | Brockhampton church | 1hr 45min | 4.8km (3 miles) |
| 5. Mordiford and Joan's Hill | Moon Inn, Mordiford | 2hr 30min | 7.4km (4.6 miles) |
| 6. Aconbury and Athelstan's Wood | Little Birch village hall | 2hr 45min | 7.6km (4.7 miles) |
| 7. Breinton Orchards | Breinton Springs | 1hr 30min | 5.5km (3.4 miles) |
| 8. Monnington Walk and Brobury Scar | Staunton-on-Wye village hall | 2hr 45min | 8.8km (5.5 miles) |
| 9. Merbach Hill from Bredwardine | Red Lion, Bredwardine | 2hr 45min | 7.8km (4.8 miles) |
| 10. Brilley and Whitney Court | Brilley church | 2hr | 5.9km (3.7 miles) |
| 11. Rhydspence and Red Lane | Rhydspence Inn | 3hr | 10.4km (6.5 miles) |
| 12. Cusop Hill | Cusop church | 2hr 15min | 6.4km (4 miles) |
| 13. The Begwns | Common near Crossvillog | 2hr 30min | 7.2km (4.5 miles) |
| 14. Common Bychan and Rhos Fawr | Nant-y-Gollen near Felindre | 3hr | 8.8km (5.5 miles) |
| 15. Brechfa Pool | Brechfa Pool | 2hr 45min | 8.5km (5.3 miles) |

| HIGHLIGHTS |
|---|
| Old railway line, woodland, hill fort |
| Riverside walk, medieval bridge and castle |
| Suspension bridge, Italianate church |
| Hill fort, Arts and Crafts architecture, views |
| Wildflower meadows, views, orchard |
| Aconbury Hill and fort, well, spring flowers |
| Apple orchards, earthworks, drove route |
| Ancient avenue of trees, river cliff |
| Medieval fishponds, views over winding river |
| Parkland, nature reserve |
| Drove route, half-timbered inn |
| Churchyard, views, Cusop Dingle |
| Moorland common, mountain views, pond |
| Upland commons, birdlife |
| Views, lake with rare plants and birdlife |

# SYMBOLS USED ON ROUTE MAPS

 Start point

 Finish point

 Start and finish at the same place

**4** → Waypoint

 Route line

## MAPPING IS SHOWN AT A SCALE OF 1:25,000

| 0 KM | 0.25 | 0.5 |
|---|---|---|

| 0 miles | | 0.25 |

## DOWNLOAD THE GPX FILES FREE AT

cicerone.co.uk/1289/gpx

*Walking towards Capodolwyn (Walk 12)*

# INTRODUCTION

*The Wye at the Warren near Hay*

Widely considered to be the most beautiful river in England and Wales, the River Wye changes character repeatedly and dramatically along its journey from Plynlimon in the Cambrian Mountains to Chepstow on the Severn estuary. The middle section of the river covered in this book may no longer be the tumbling mountain stream of the upper reaches, nor yet the mature lowland river hemmed in by a limestone gorge, but it has a beguiling character and offers walkers a sensational variety of top-quality experiences.

The landscapes of the middle Wye, from Llyswen just above Hay-on-Wye to Goodrich downstream from Ross-on-Wye, are superb. Highlights include the upland commons of Brechfa and the Begwns, the lower slopes of the Black Mountains and, further downstream, the lush farmland of the Herefordshire plain with its strikingly rich red soils. And the countryside is alive with birds such as skylarks, yellowhammers and redstarts, especially in summer, while buzzards and red kites patrol the skies above.

## Walking in the Wye valley

Walkers in the Wye valley have an array of fabulous routes to choose from, ranging from easy walking on riverside

*The summit slopes of Merbach Hill (Walk 9)*

paths to enjoyable tramps along some of the region's many drove roads, including those at Breinton (Walk 7) and Rhydspence (Walk 11). Around Hay-on-Wye the wide green tracks across upland commons are a special treat, while south of Hereford the river itself forms a constant and delightful backdrop to many of the walks.

Signposting of footpaths and bridleways in the Welsh borders is almost always very good, and the terrain is such that it is generally easy to follow the routes in this book, which are all circular and make use of the superb network of paths and tracks in the southern part of the Welsh Marches.

A number of long-distance paths cross the middle reaches of the Wye, and routes in this book utilise parts of the Offa's Dyke Path, a spectacular route which traverses the Welsh border between Chepstow and Prestatyn, the Wye Valley Walk, which traces the river from source to sea, and the Herefordshire Trail, an enjoyable circular route taking in many of the highlights of the county's countryside.

## Special things to see

The River Wye, of course, takes centre stage, especially when seen from one of the bridges which span the water – perhaps the striking pedestrian suspension bridge at Sellack Boat (Walk 3) or the attractive multi-arched medieval bridge at Wilton (Walk 2). The tree-lined river in a broad floodplain exudes pastoral tranquillity and there are cider apple orchards galore, for example at Breinton and Bredwardine (Walks 7 and 9), as well as hidden gems, including the Woolhope Dome (Walk 5) with its intricate pattern of abrupt ridges and tiny valleys.

The scenery is varied and impressive, whether intimate in scale like The Prospect in Ross (Walk 2) or the outstanding tree-lined avenue at Monnington-on-Wye (Walk 8), or remarkably extensive, taking in the

Black Mountain foothills or astonishing panoramas from modest heights such as Mynydd Forest (Walk 15) or Merbach Hill (Walk 9).

The historic environment, too, is special. There are Iron Age settlements on Aconbury Hill and at Capler Camp (Walks 4 and 6), Norman castles at King's Caple and Cusop (Walks 3 and 12), medieval fishponds at Bredwardine (Walk 9) and a series of exquisite churches, including Llanelieu with its astonishing rood screen (Walk 14) and the 18th-century Italianate gem at Hoarwithy (Walk 3).

## Bases and places to stay

Three very different towns compete for attention: the county town of Hereford, its cathedral renowned for its chained library and Mappa Mundi; the bustling market town of Ross-on-Wye; and the border stronghold of Hay-on-Wye, famous for its numerous second-hand bookshops and the gateway to the upper Wye.

The largest and most central of the urban centres in the area, Hereford has a variety of accommodation options together with a wide variety of shops, restaurants, pubs and cafes and makes an ideal base for exploring the middle Wye valley. Hay-on-Wye also has plenty of rooms (but avoid the book festival period!), and in the south Ross-on-Wye is very conveniently located for several of the walks. There is also a choice of inns and bed-and-breakfast options in the villages.

## Travel

Accessible from the M4 and M5 via the A40 or A4103, Hereford has direct trains from London, Birmingham, Manchester and Cardiff, while Ross-on-Wye and Hay-on-Wye can be reached by bus from Gloucester and Hereford respectively.

Local buses connect Hereford with Ross-on-Wye, Mordiford, Staunton-on-Wye and Hay-on-Wye, and Ross has a service from Gloucester together with buses to Hoarwithy. The villages around Hay are poorly served by public transport, but local bus services can be used to access several of the walks using public transport.

The riverside path back to Ross-on-Wye (Walk 2)

*The way through the coast redwoods*

# WALK 1
## Chase Wood from Ross-on-Wye

**Time** 1hr 30min
**Distance** 4.2km (2.6 miles)
**Climb** 150m

**A stroll along a railway line followed by easy woodland walking by the ramparts of a hill fort, with one stiff climb**

| | |
|---|---|
| **Start/finish** | Fernbank Road, Ross-on-Wye |
| **Locate** | ///expressed.goat.erupted |
| **Cafes/pubs** | Selection in Ross town centre (1km from start) |
| **Transport** | Infrequent service on bus 35 from Ross to Monmouth |
| **Parking** | Small car park on Fernbank Road, signposted Town and Country Trail from B4234 (HR9 5PP) |
| **Toilets** | No public toilets on route |

Chase Wood dominates the skyline south of Ross-on-Wye, but the summit plateau provides easy walking through a variety of woodland environments, including a stand of giant coast redwoods. The hill fort that once enclosed the summit is now a huge upland pasture defended by a single rampart. The return to Ross includes tremendous views to the Welsh hills, including the Skirrid and the Sugar Loaf.

*The view back over Ross from above Alton Court*

**1** Walk through the little car park to find and follow the old railway line, at first on a wide track through a cutting. *Heavily loss-making, the Ross and Monmouth railway closed to passengers in 1959.* The path narrows, now with houses to the left and a fine view across fields to Chase Wood on the right. Cross a footpath and then angle down to meet Penyard Lane.

**2** Turn right (signposted Wye Valley Walk) and pass **Alton Court** Farm and an activity holiday complex. The tarmac ends and the route lies through a gate onto a good path running through woodland, with a small quarry to the right. Go through a second gate and immediately turn right – unsignposted – to climb steadily on an obvious path

towards a mobile phone mast. Turn right again as the slope eases to reach a field gate at the edge of **Alton Court Wood**.

**3** Go through the gate onto an excellent track, gradually gaining height before emerging from the wood onto an open plateau, with the summit of Chase Wood straight ahead beyond **Hill Farm**. Go through a kissing gate onto a path through **Merrivale Wood**, passing to the right of the farm and

*ⓘ Designated as a Special Area of Conservation, the Wye is important for Atlantic salmon, pearl mussels, white-clawed crayfish and a variety of plants.*

*The old railway path from Fernbank Road*

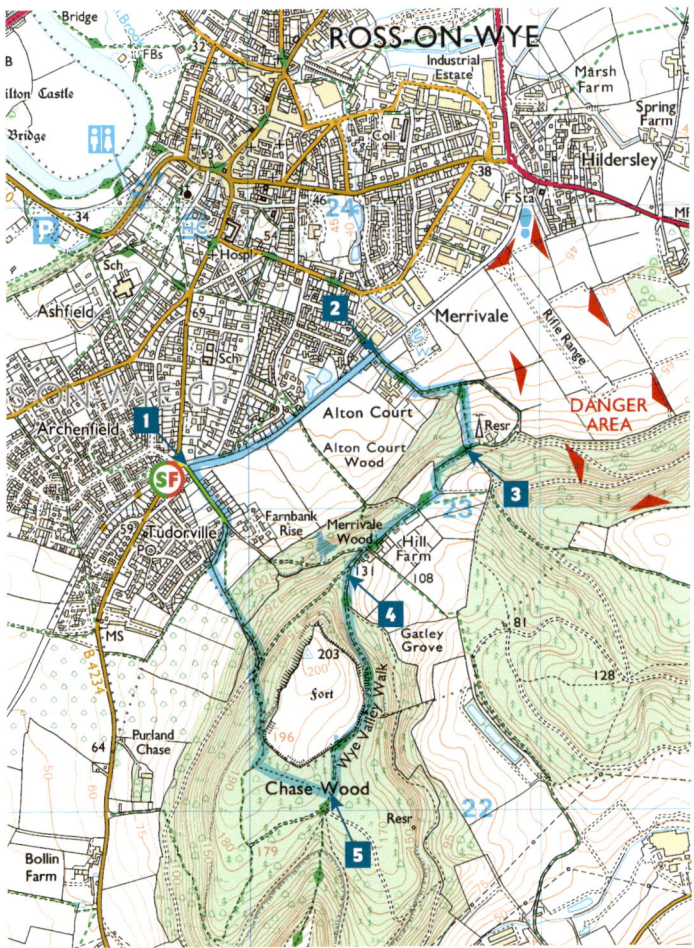

climbing steadily on a gravel track. **Merrivale Wood is a local nature reserve with abundant birdlife and butterflies in ancient woodland** **above Ross.** Go past a barrier and then take the left fork, still following the Wye Valley Walk.

*The massive interior of the hill fort, its ancient ramparts cloaked in trees*

**4** The wide gravelly track continues uphill, with steep slopes looming above to the right. As the slope eases the ramparts of the **Chase Wood** hill fort come into view. Ignore a locked gate to the right, continuing on the track to reach a path junction where a footpath is signposted to the right.

> ⓘ *The Wye, Britain's fourth longest river, runs 250km from its source on Plynlimon in mid Wales to Chepstow on the Severn estuary.*

**An Iron Age fort with a single rampart, Chase Wood hill fort encloses an area of 11 hectares. A camp rather than a true defensive structure, it was occupied over a prolonged period of time, with perhaps 1400 inhabitants at times.**

**5** Turn right to follow a clear path as it winds through an impressive stand of coast redwoods, keep right at a junction and fork left after a further 75m, just before the path approaches the southern boundary of the hill fort. The way lies steeply downhill at first, with a short flight of wooden steps aiding the descent towards a forest road. Turn right here, then left after 20m onto a narrow woodland path which eventually emerges into a field above suburban Ross-on-Wye, with the Welsh hills in the distance. Keep ahead across the field and turn right alongside houses to reach Fernbank Road and return to the car park.

# WALK 2
## Ross-on-Wye and Wilton

| | |
|---|---|
| **Start/finish** | *Market House, Ross-on-Wye* |
| **Locate** | *///onto.potato.interview* |
| **Cafes/pubs** | *Wide choice in Ross-on-Wye* |
| **Transport** | *Buses from Gloucester, Hereford and Monmouth* |
| **Parking** | *Several car parks (fee payable) in town* |
| **Toilets** | *Croft Court shopping centre (200m from the Market House)* |

**Time** 2hr
**Distance** 5.8km (3.6 miles)
**Climb** 50m

**A historic market town, an easy riverside walk and a medieval bridge and castle**

The countryside immediately south-west of Ross-on-Wye provides a varied walk, starting with the town's church precinct and magnificent views over the river from the open space of The Prospect. Riverside walking follows, alongside the shallow Wye with its gravel beds, followed by the medieval castle and bridge in Wilton and a stretch of riverside parkland enlivened by superb sculptures.

The River Wye below Wilton bridge

*Looking back along the path near Lower Cleeve Farm*

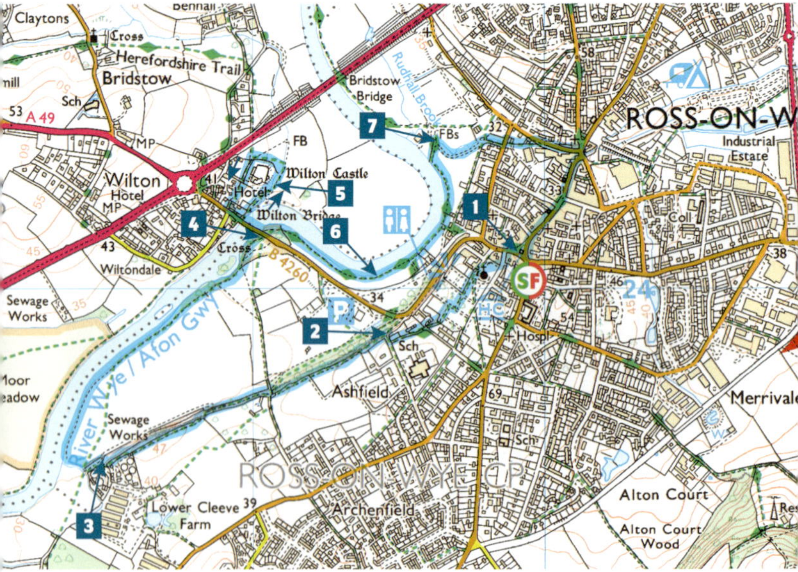

**1** Take High Street alongside the Market House and turn left into Church Street, passing the 16th-century Rudhall Almshouses and turning right into the churchyard. Cut diagonally across to the **church**, walk past the entrance to The Prospect, and zigzag right and left through the extensive graveyard, following signposts for the John Kyrle Walk. Leave the churchyard on a tarmac path between fences, passing **Ashfield** school playing fields, then swing left and immediately right when the tarmac ends, and turn left after 25m onto a narrow path.

**2** The path runs above a cliff falling away towards the floodplain of the River Wye. The way then lies through two large arable fields. Fork right just before the end of the second field to descend a flight of steps. Go straight across a sunken lane, up steps and along a delightful path under trees, then follow the right-hand edge of an arable field, with **Lower Cleeve Farm** ahead to the left. Drop down to the right to emerge unexpectedly in a prairie landscape of huge fields on the flood plain.

**3** Aim for a prominent signpost 200m to the left, turning right here and curving sharply round to follow the river. The long trek around the field edge includes several opportunities to drop down to the gravel beds in the river channel, with swans and herons close by and Wilton bridge ahead. Pass sports pitches and then fork left to arrive at steps leading up to the main road into Ross.

*Wilton bridge*

**4** Turn left across the superb **Wilton bridge**. Dating from 1597, the bridge has six round arches and an 18th-century sundial. Drop down to the right onto a riverside footpath, overgrown in summer, which leads through a gate to an open area with an excellent view of Wilton Castle, and then to a footbridge over a little stream.

**The red sandstone Wilton Castle, dating partly from the 14th century and partly from the Elizabethan era, was burnt by the Royalists in the Civil War after its owner, Sir John Brydges, refused to let them use it as a base.**

*Wilton Castle*

*The Market House in Ross-on-Wye*

**5** Cross the stream and turn left across a second footbridge, circling around the castle to find a kissing gate giving access to an enclosed path back to the main road. Go left here, re-crossing Wilton bridge, and immediately drop down to follow the popular riverside path as far as a sculpture of mallards in flight.

*Walenty Pytel's Mallards sculpture*

The mallard sculpture is by internationally acclaimed sculptor Walenty Pytel. Pytel was born in Poland but has long lived in Herefordshire. His work using sheet metal is inspired by the natural environment.

**6** Continue along the riverside path through the Hope and Anchor pleasure gardens and past the boat launch, then take the tarmac track through parkland with a spectacular swan sculpture as far as the entrance to Ross rowing club.

**7** Turn right here and go straight on along a lane to reach and cross Trenchard Street. Take the footpath, signposted to the town centre, alongside a canalised stream, continue along Greytree Road and then turn sharp right to climb up Brookend Street back to the Market House.

## Ross-on-Wye

Now a bustling market town, Ross-on-Wye was an important base for late 18th-century tourists who took the Wye Tour by boat along the river in search of picturesque scenery, medieval ruins and early industry. The town owes much to John Kyrle, the 'Man of Ross', who laid out The Prospect pleasure gardens in 1693. St Mary's Church has an impressive collection of monuments, while the Market House, dominating the centre of town, dates from the 1660s.

*Hoarwithy village with its Italianate church*

# WALK 3
## Sellack Boat and Hoarwithy

| | |
|---|---|
| **Start/finish** | *King's Caple church* |
| **Locate** | *///overtones.truth.collected* |
| **Cafes/pubs** | *Pub in Hoarwithy* |
| **Transport** | *Limited service from Ross-on-Wye* |
| **Parking** | *Roadside parking near church (HR1 4TX)* |
| **Toilets** | *No public toilets on route* |

**Time** 2hr 45min
**Distance** 8.2km (5.1 miles)
**Climb** 125m

**An easy and popular walk through classic English lowland scenery, visiting three quite different villages**

This classic and well-used route on clear footpaths and country lanes goes from King's Caple, with its castle motte, to the ornate pedestrian suspension bridge over the River Wye at Sellack Boat. This is followed by riverside walking below Castlemeadow Wood, a superb path above Red Rail and past the shrunken hamlet of Llanfrother, and finally the remarkable Italianate church at Hoarwithy.

*The path across the water meadows from Sellack*

**1** Head east from the church, with the castle earthworks opposite. *The only surviving remnant of King's Caple castle is the steep-sided circular motte.* Pass King's Caple Court and carry straight on at a crossroads with the tiny former Victorian Sunday and day school on the corner. After 300m turn right onto a footpath between tall hedges and pass through two gates to cross a big arable field to a stile. Turn right along a narrow lane, then left when the road bends right, using a rough track to reach the river at the **Sellack Boat** pedestrian bridge.

**2** Cross the bridge – its wooden planks are somewhat worn in places – and follow an obvious path which leads straight across **Sellack Common** towards Sellack church. *This is the only English church dedicated to St Tysilio, who lived in Wales in the 7th century.* Just before the church a path heads over a stile and below Castlemeadow Wood, crossing water

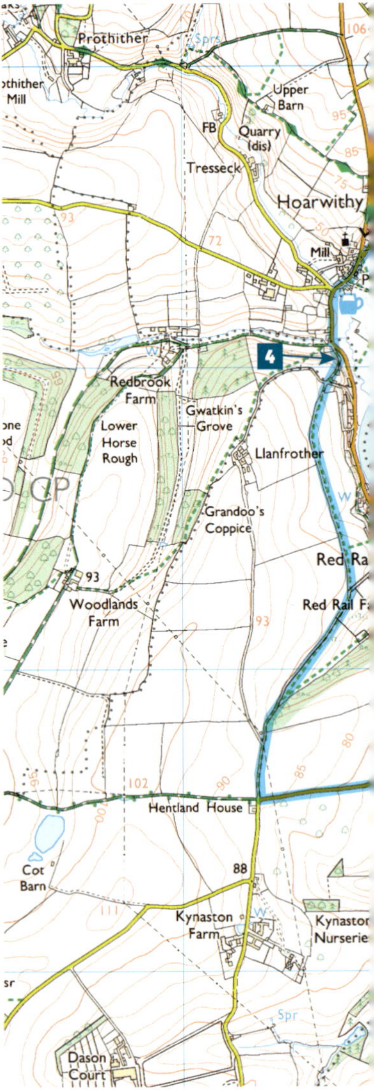

*The suspension footbridge at Sellack Boat*

meadows and gradually reaching then following the riverbank. Finally the path curves left to reach the road at **Sheppon Hill Stables**.

**3** Cross the road and climb the lane towards Kynaston, then turn right before Hentland House onto a track and turn right again below a huge electricity pylon onto a green lane. Cross a stile and keep straight ahead over a farm road above **Red Rail**, with outstanding views across the Wye to the church spires at Kings Caple and Sellack. To the left is Llanfrother, once the site of a 6th-century monastic college and a medieval hamlet, now deserted. The way now lies down a woodland path to join the road on the southern outskirts of **Hoarwithy**, with the Church of St Catherine soon in view ahead.

Hoarwithy church is well worth a visit. It was rebuilt in the 1880s in a flamboyant Italianate style, with a campanile, a cloister walk with fine mosaic pavements, Byzantine capitals in the apse and a stained-glass window by the Pre-Raphaelite artist Edward Burne-Jones.

**4** Keep on the road past the New Harp Inn, but just before the entrance to the church take the lane on the right, signposted to King's Caple. This leads quickly to **Hoarwithy bridge**. Cross the bridge, passing the former tollhouse on the west bank of the river. The tollhouse accompanied the first timber bridge here, which replaced a ford and ferry in 1856.

*Spectacular views above Red Rail*

*The old tollhouse by Hoarwithy bridge*

**5** Turn right onto a grassy path which hugs the riverbank in places and emerges onto a little lane at **Ruxton**. Follow the lane as it swings left, passing the driveway to Pennoxstone Court, and follows the line of Caple Street, once a minor Roman road, to arrive back at the church and castle mound at **King's Caple**.

> ⓘ *The churches at King's Caple, Sellack and Hentland distribute pax cakes with the blessing 'peace and good neighbourhood' after the Palm Sunday service (on the Sunday before Easter).*

## Sellack Boat

The pedestrian suspension bridge at Sellack Boat is the best surviving example from the celebrated Louis Harper foundry at Craiginches in Aberdeen. It was built in 1895 at the instigation of the vicar of Sellack to replace a ferry whose wilful boatman had repeatedly refused to row him and his parishioners across the river. A previous vicar had resorted to crossing the river on stilts to avoid this problem.

*Timber stacking areas in Capler Wood*

# WALK 4
## Capler Camp

| | |
|---|---|
| **Start/finish** | *Brockhampton church* |
| **Locate** | *///ferrying.nurses.cricket* |
| **Cafes/pubs** | *None on route* |
| **Transport** | *No public transport* |
| **Parking** | *Limited roadside parking by church (HR1 4SD), alternative parking at Waypoint 3* |
| **Toilets** | *No public toilets on route* |

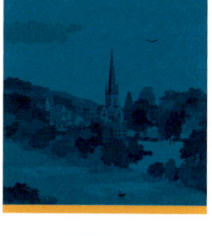

**Time** 1hr 45min
**Distance** 4.8km (3 miles)
**Climb** 110m

**A stunning route packed with interest, following superb paths and clear woodland tracks**

Using a mixture of clear footpaths and green lanes, this exceptional walk includes the thatched Brockhampton church, a renowned view across the Wye from Capler Lodge, and Capler Camp, a spectacular Iron Age fort enclosing a massive area with double ramparts. The walking is easy, with only one gradual climb, and an extensive outlook southwards from the hill fort to the Forest of Dean.

*Marcle Ridge from the trig point above Camp Farm*

*Descending the dry valley from Brockhampton*

**1** From the gate opposite **Brockhampton church** a delightful footpath marked by tall, inscribed posts makes its way down a glorious, grassy dry valley flanked by woodland. Brockhampton Court, glimpsed to the left, was once an hotel but is now a care home. Turn right onto a narrow winding lane, and right again to follow another road for 200m to a signposted track on the left.

**2** Follow the track, part of the Wye Valley Walk, as it runs between hazel and hawthorn hedges. Go straight on at a crossroads of footpaths, then turn right by a big oak tree to follow the left-hand hedge of an enormous field as far as a country lane at **Brinkley Hill**. Go straight across the road onto a gravelly track, passing an isolated cottage with steep slopes on the left, to rejoin the road at the **Capler Lodge** viewpoint.

*Intricate bench at the Capler Lodge viewpoint*

**3** Head past the little parking area and Capler Lodge, then veer right onto a stony track, climbing steadily through the open deciduous woodland of **Capler Wood**. Fork right after a timber stacking area onto a green path through conifers, right again onto a broad track, and right again to reach a hand gate on the edge of **Capler Camp**. Follow the path along the ditch between the two southern ramparts of the hill fort towards a big stone barn. The inner rampart rises impressively to the left, complemented by a wide panorama to the right that includes May Hill and the northern scarp of the Forest of Dean.

**4** Turn right immediately after the barn and take the track which crests the little hill, passes a trig point and reaches a gate onto a gravelly lane.

*The path through the ramparts of Capler Camp*

Walk between a house and its outbuildings, then go slightly to the left to locate a path across a field to a kissing gate. Head diagonally left to a second kissing gate, go round the right-hand side of the third field to a stile by a tall wooden post, and take the obvious path across a final field to a gate. Walk down the lane through **Brand Oak** to the road and turn right to return to Brockhampton church, which is well worth a visit.

The thatched All Saints Church at Brockhampton is a magnificent example of the early 20th-century Arts and Crafts movement, with two towers (one with a pyramid roof), steeply pointed arches in the nave and chancel, and tapestries by Edward Burne-Jones.

## Capler Camp

The Iron Age hill fort at Capler Camp has a double rampart for much of its circumference, with ditches that are cut into the rock on the steeper north side of the fort. Evidence of later occupation includes the foundations of a 17th-century house. The hill fort covers an area of around 6 hectares. Well known for its ash, oak and lime woodland and its display of bluebells in May, the fort is also home to fallow deer and a range of woodland birds.

# WALK 5
## Mordiford and Joan's Hill

**Time** 2hr 30min
**Distance** 7.4km
(4.6 miles)
**Climb** 220m

**An outstanding walk with fine views, a hill fort and hay meadows brimming with orchids in summer**

| | |
|---|---|
| **Start/finish** | Moon Inn, Mordiford |
| **Locate** | ///onlookers.brand.carver |
| **Cafes/pubs** | Pub in Mordiford |
| **Transport** | Bus 453 provides a basic service from Hereford to Mordiford |
| **Parking** | Limited roadside parking in village |
| **Toilets** | No public toilets on route |

This is an amazingly varied route, including old tracks, wildflower meadows, woodland and upland pastures, with outstanding views both to the west and into the Woolhope Dome. Backbury Hill with its Iron Age fort, the nature reserve at Joan's Hill Farm and the interesting village of Mordiford are among the highlights. There are several reminders on the walk of the Mordiford Dragon, which supposedly devoured animals and people before being confronted by a man in a barrel!

*A delivery of local cider to the Moon Inn*

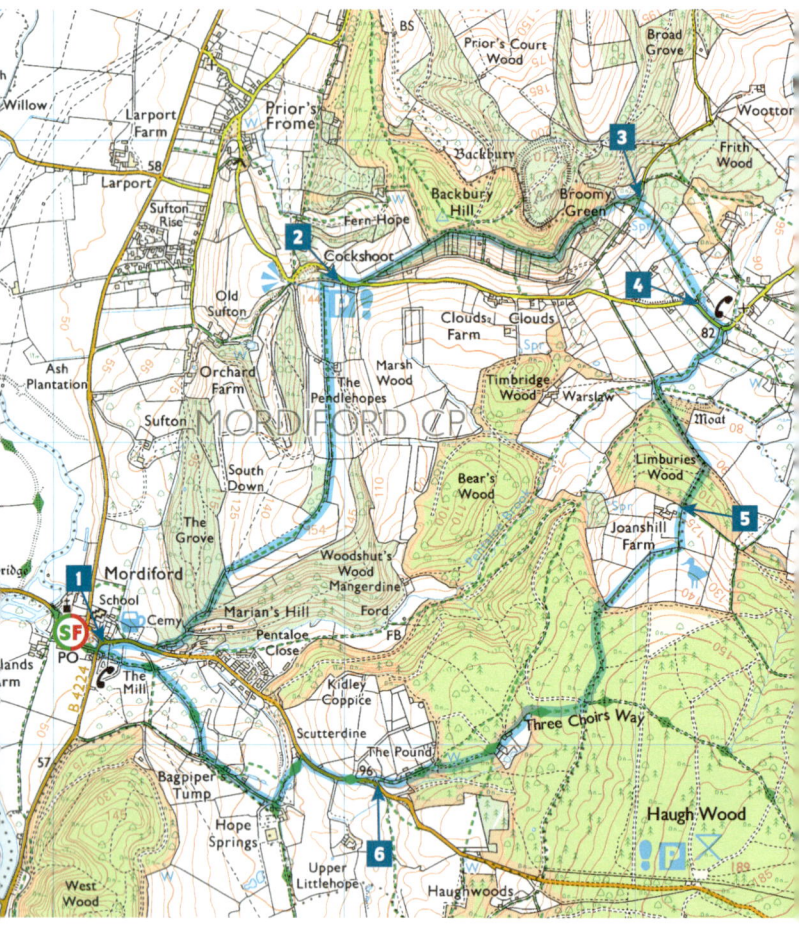

**1** Use the tarmac footpath that runs alongside the Woolhope road from the Moon Inn, passing the cemetery before turning left, uphill, on a lane before Lower Rock Cottage. Turn left again onto a path heading steeply uphill through **The Grove**, leaving the woodland through a gate and keeping to the right-hand side of a big pasture. Keep to the right of a copse to find a superb

*The path through Jay's Orchard*

green lane past **The Pendlehopes** – ruined buildings now home to a picnic site – then turn right to reach a country lane.

**2** Leave the lane to the left after 75m, then immediately fork left again on a rising path worn to the bedrock in places, climbing the slopes of **Backbury Hill**. Turn right at a

*Wildflower meadows below Backbury Hill*

crossroads of paths, now on a wide path through woodland with small fields to the right. The summit of Backbury Hill lies straight on at the crossroads, with the hill fort a little further away. The path descends gradually to a junction; turn left here on a gravelly track to reach a T-junction.

**3** Go right on a wide stony lane, then quickly left onto a delightful footpath passing through two gates to reach the first of two hay meadows. The many wildflowers in these meadows include buttercups, lady's slipper, yarrow and speedwell. A clear path winds through the meadows and then a gate leads to a quiet lane.

**4** Swing left along the lane towards **Checkley**, then turn right after 150m onto a narrow path alongside a brook. It is worth a short detour to visit the hamlet of Checkley, with its black-and-white farmhouses. The way lies through two more wildflower meadows, with buttercups and pignut in profusion, then over two stiles to reach a gravelly lane. Turn left and stay on the lane as it rises slightly through **Limburies Wood** then swings right, uphill, to reach farm buildings at Joan's Hill Farm Nature Reserve.

A former working farm now owned by conservation charity Plantlife, the nature reserve has several unimproved hay meadows and orchards which are home to thousands of orchids in May and June, together with lady's bed-straw and many other flowers.

**5** Turn left through a field gate, then keep right through the orchard, an integral part of the Joan's Hill reserve. Go through a gap in the hedge at the end of the orchard and through two more meadows to find an outsized kissing gate leading into Haugh Wood. A clear path winds through the wood, passing massive mounds teeming with wood ants. Cross a forest road but turn immediately right down steps onto the **Three Choirs Way**, the path sunken at times until it follows a track down to a road.

**6** Go right along the road for 250m, taking the second left turn alongside Iron House. The roughly surfaced lane swings left past limekilns and the access path to Scutterdine Quarry. Turn right before converted farm buildings, now on a tarmacked lane until a track drops down to the right at **Bagpiper's Tump** and reaches Jay's Orchard. By a gate into the orchard you pass a barrel containing Garstone, who reputedly confronted and vanquished the Mordiford dragon. A superb path runs through the orchard and then crosses a foot-bridge to a track leading past **Mordiford Mill** and over the Pentaloe Brook to the Moon Inn.

Joan's Hill farmhouse

Jay's Orchard is named after George Jay, who was a small-holder and Prudential insurance agent. The traditional orchard, with sheep grazing under the trees, contains 40 varieties of cider apple and perry pear trees.

Garstone in his barrel near Bagpiper's Tump

*Aconbury from the upper fishpond*

# WALK 6
## Aconbury and Athelstan's Wood

**Time** 2h 45min
**Distance** 7.6km
(4.7 miles)
**Climb** 225m

**Woodland walking, open countryside with wide views, a hill fort and an ancient well**

| | |
|---|---|
| **Start/finish** | *Little Birch village hall* |
| **Locate** | *///toward.pampered.papers* |
| **Cafes/pubs** | *None on route* |
| **Transport** | *Bus 33 between Hereford and Ross-on-Wye calls hourly at King's Thorn (1km west of start)* |
| **Parking** | *Limited parking at village hall, donation requested (HR2 8AZ)* |
| **Toilets** | *No public toilets on route* |

An exhilarating walk on woodland tracks and well-marked footpaths, visiting a hill fort hidden in bracken, a former nunnery church and a substantial old well. The descent to Aconbury features an outstanding panorama over Hereford and its cathedral, while the woodlands are carpeted in spring with bluebells, ramsons and anemones. Quiet lanes and green tracks complete the return through the scattered settlement of Little Birch.

*The clear path heading towards Aconbury Court*

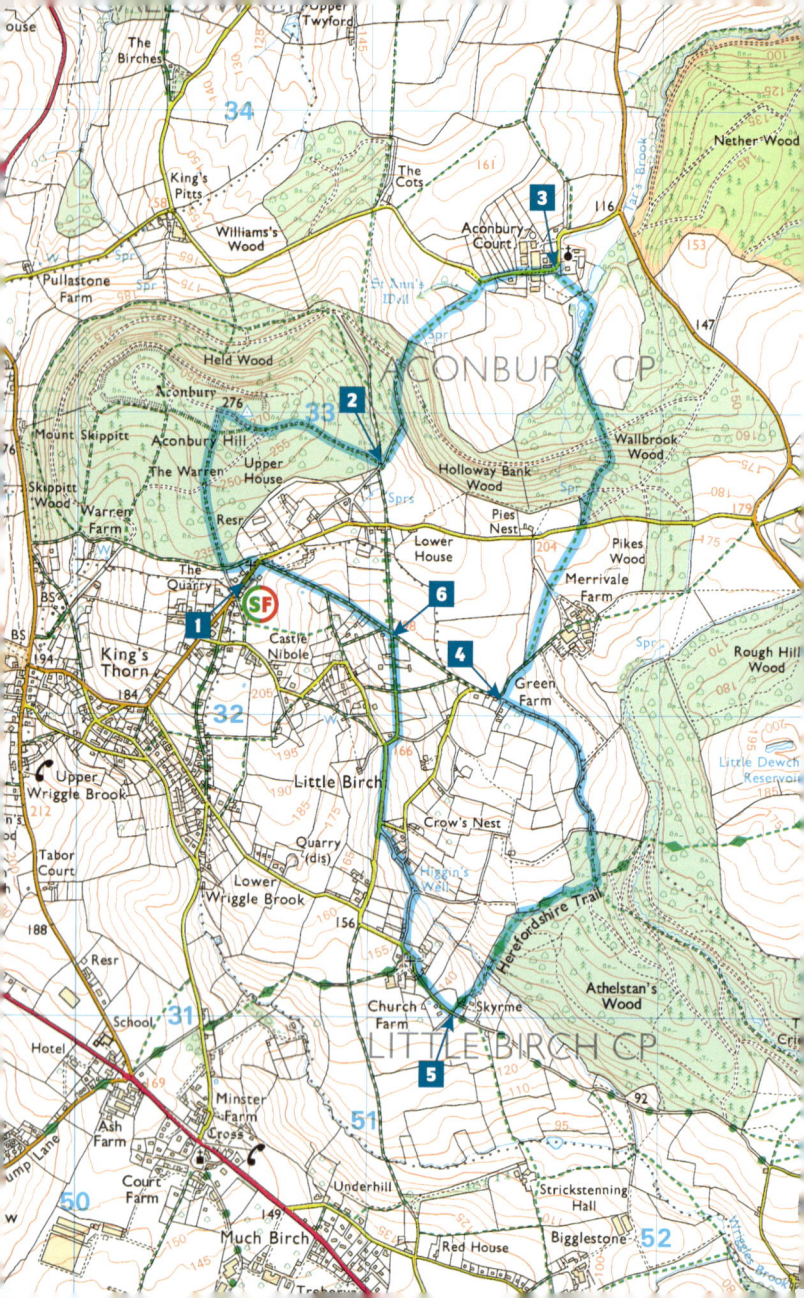

**1** From the village hall cross the road (Barrack Hill) to the former Primitive Methodist chapel and turn sharp left onto a green lane, passing an old water pump. Turn right through a gate by an information panel and take the wide path straight ahead, climbing very gently through coppiced chestnuts. Ignore paths to the right and left to arrive at a T-junction at the southern ramparts of the hill fort on **Aconbury Hill**.

The hill fort encircling the summit of Aconbury Hill dates from the Iron Age. Its ramparts and ditches enclose an area of 7 hectares. The fort was reused as a lookout by Parliamentarian forces during the English Civil War.

ⓘ *Hillforts such as those at Capler Camp and Aconbury are reminders of past border disputes in the Welsh Marches.*

Turn right on a clear path, fork right and then left, and swing left again when a more substantial path comes in from the right. Follow this path, signposted as a public footpath, across several junctions to reach the woodland edge.

**2** Go over a stile into a field with wide views to May Hill and the Cotswolds, turn left to reach another stile, and drop down to turn briefly right on a gravelly track, then left on a narrow path which quickly reaches a

*Cider press by Aconbury Court*

*Springtime in Athelstan's Wood*

big arable field. Cross the field on a very obvious path, with a great prospect ahead of Dinedor Hill and Hereford, then turn right along a country lane to arrive at a cider press outside **Aconbury Court**.

> **The church at Aconbury, long disused, was part of an Augustinian nunnery, and has blocked doorways and windows which once led into the cloisters. The present Aconbury Court is the successor to a 16th-century mansion house with walled gardens.**

**3** Take the footpath by the cider press, passing between two attractive fishponds and swinging right to climb along the right-hand edge of a big field. Take the track into woodland, cross a gravelly road and head steeply up into **Wallbrook Wood**, the route well signposted and finally curving left to meet a minor road. Keep straight ahead over the road and go across two fields to join an enclosed grassy lane heading for **Green Farm**.

**4** Turn left to find an excellent green lane which leads into **Athelstan's Wood**. The wood, famous for its springtime anemones, was owned by the Bishops of Hereford for several centuries. Turn right on reaching a wider track and follow Herefordshire Trail waymarks through coppiced woodland and across Wriggles Brook to the hamlet of **Skyrme**.

**5** Go past St Mary's Church, then take the rough track on the right to drop down into the Wriggles Brook valley again, this time passing **Higgin's Well**. Dating from the early 19th century, the well was restored in 1897 to commemorate Queen Victoria's diamond jubilee. Take the often muddy lane ahead, turn right onto a country lane and fork right after 300m onto School Lane to reach a junction of paths and tracks.

**6** Turn left onto the lane known locally as Chapel Pitch, which quickly becomes a delightful green lane, narrows to a footpath and finally becomes a stony track as it reaches Barrack Hill by the Methodist chapel. Turn left to return to the village hall.

## – To shorten

Turn right at Waypoint 4 and follow Chapel Pitch in a direct line back to the former Methodist chapel, saving 2.3km (50min).

Higgin's Well

*The track through orchards south of Wyevale Wood*

# WALK 7
## Breinton Orchards

**Time** 1hr 30min
**Distance** 5.5km (3.4 miles)
**Climb** 55m

| | |
|---|---|
| **Start/finish** | *Breinton Springs car park* |
| **Locate** | *///assess.painting.tensions* |
| **Cafes/pubs** | *None on route* |
| **Transport** | *No public transport* |
| **Parking** | *Small National Trust car park (HR4 7PG)* |
| **Toilets** | *No public toilets on route* |

**A gentle stroll around apple orchards, passing medieval earthworks and a freshwater spring by the riverside**

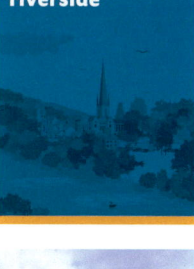

This is an easy and largely level route, passing through dessert and cider apple orchards, some quite old and others recently planted. Highlights include a freshwater spring on a small cliff by the river, medieval earthworks reputed to be those of the country retreat of the treasurer of Hereford Cathedral, and part of the Green Lane drove route heading for Hereford and London.

*Earthworks by Breinton church*

**1** Before you begin the walk drop down from the car park to view the medieval earthworks in the field by the church, together with the spring by the riverside; then return to the start and take the narrow lane past Breinton House, its gate pillars topped by enormous sculptures of deer. Described in 1916 as 'exceedingly picturesque', Breinton House had kitchen gardens, orchards, tennis and croquet lawns and riverside walks. Just beyond a minor lane take the path through a metal gate into an orchard, and then cross a lane onto a stony track, quickly reaching a wooden kissing gate.

**2** Turn left and follow the hedge through two fields, eventually descending a flight of steps to reach and turn right on a country road. Go left at a junction, passing a mailbox hidden in the hedge, and swing right to walk past the attractively half-timbered South View. Turn left onto a rough track just past South View,

passing **Manor House**. The track narrows between hedges and climbs to cross a field. *From here there are spectacular views of Aconbury Hill to the south and the massif of the Black Mountains ahead.* Traverse one more field before arriving at a gate.

**3** Go through the gate but immediately turn sharp right over a stile onto a narrow path through woodland, with a steep slope to the left. The path emerges into an overgrown pasture; go straight ahead and follow the narrow path through a second, much bigger field, eventually dropping down over a stile into an old orchard at **Upper Wood**. Wind past an ancient hedgerow and through the orchard to find a stile tucked away in the right-hand corner. A narrow path runs briefly through woodland, then swings left to follow the field boundary to a road junction.

**4** Keep straight ahead down a met-alled lane, now on the Green Lane drove route.

*Deer on the gatepost of Breinton House*

**Green Lane was once part of a drove route which connected Mid Wales with markets in Hereford and London. Drovers Pond once provided water for the animals on their way to market.**

The lane is unexpectedly sub-urban, passing bungalows and the entrance to a **caravan park**, but the way forward quickly narrows, becom-ing a narrow path in a broad but

*Looking back along the path as it reaches Upper Wood*

largely overgrown corridor. Turn right at a crossroads of paths at the corner of **Wyevale Wood**. The Wyevale Wood Nature Reserve, on an ancient woodland site, boasts great spotted woodpeckers and nuthatches. The route is now on a good grassy path which runs alongside orchards to reach a country lane.

**5** Head straight across the lane, following the left-hand hedgerow across two fields to rejoin the outward route at the wooden kissing gate. Take the path alongside a cottage, go diagonally through the orchard and walk down the lane to the Breinton Springs car park.

### ✚ To lengthen

Take the path from the car park to Warham House, returning along the riverside and past Breinton Springs, adding 2.4km (40min) to the walk.

## Breinton Springs

Owned by the National Trust, this is a delightfully intimate landscape with a traditional orchard (many of the trees now over-mature), and a medieval mound associated with the treasurer of Hereford Cathedral. There is also a trackway to a ford defended by the Mercians in the 8th century and later used by cattle drovers, and a freshwater spring emerging just above the river.

# WALK 8

## Monnington Walk and Brobury Scar

**Time** 2hr 45min
**Distance** 8.8km (5.5 miles)
**Climb** 90m

**Easy walking on green paths through cider apple orchards and along a historic avenue of pines and yews**

| | |
|---|---|
| **Start/finish** | *Staunton-on-Wye village hall* |
| **Locate** | *///fittingly.uppermost.prancing* |
| **Cafes/pubs** | *Pub at Staunton (restricted opening hours)* |
| **Transport** | *A few buses a day from Hereford* |
| **Parking** | *At village hall (HR4 7LR)* |
| **Toilets** | *No public toilets on route* |

The centrepiece of this superb route is Monnington Walk, a mile-long avenue of yew and pine trees originally planted in 1623, which runs north-west from Monnington Court to finish above Brobury Scar, a red sandstone cliff rising 30m above the Wye. The path also cuts through a succession of cider apple orchards and visits the extraordinary church at Monnington.

*The river near Monnington-on-Wye*

**1** Walk to the New Inn and take the lane to its right to emerge into a field. Turn left along a fenced green walkway, climb a stile and go through a gate at the end of a second field to find a track between polytunnels and a tall hedge. The track leads to the yard of **Oakchurch Farm**, but take a green lane just before this on the right, which emerges onto a road. Turn left, then take the narrow tarmac path through a gate straight ahead to reach the village church.

**2** Go round the church to find a kissing gate leading to a roughly surfaced lane, and follow this through two fields, dropping down to cross a stile onto a hidden path through trees. Keep straight ahead across two fields to locate a hole in the far hedge which leads to a quiet country lane. Turn right here to reach the **Portway Hotel**.

**3** Cross the busy A438 onto Monnington Lane, turning left after 250m onto a signposted footpath. Follow the waymarked path as it zigzags through several cider apple orchards, eventually swinging right with the **Maddle Brook** alongside to reach and cross a footbridge in the left-hand hedge.

**4** Go straight ahead, now on the Wye Valley Walk, then turn right on reaching the riverbank. As the river bends

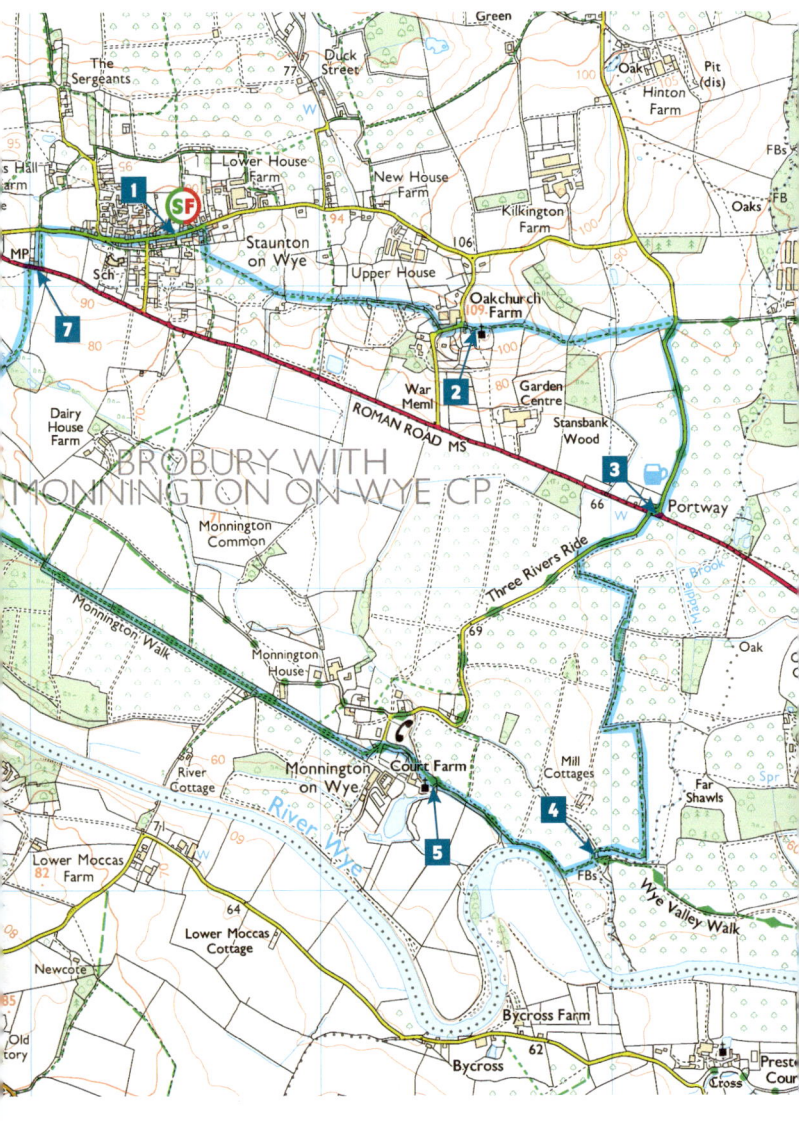

*Skirting a cider apple orchard alongside Maddle Brook*

left, walk straight ahead between an orchard and an open field with the tower of **Monnington-on-Wye** church ahead. A path leads left into the churchyard, with the river some distance away.

**5** Leave the churchyard on a pleasant path alongside a brook. Cross a driveway and walk past a redbrick house to reach the start of the superb **Monnington Walk**. The way ahead is a wide green avenue between pines and yews. Take a slight right at the end of the walk, following a bridleway on the edge of **Monnington Coppy** wood, with Dairy House Farm to the right, to reach to a junction of paths.

*Looking back along Monnington Walk to Monnington Court*

Turn left at a gate for 100m to take in the view from the top of Brobury Scar. The red sandstone cliff was once described as 'a bold grand object amid the fine scenery of the Wye'. A ferryman took visitors across to the Moccas estate from a boathouse below the cliff.

**6** Walk along the left-hand side of a large field, with the Burton Hills on the skyline ahead. Keep ahead on a clear green track across a second field, skirt a little wood and cross a stream, then climb alongside a hedge to reach an obvious stile and cross the A438 again.

**7** Aim right of a cottage, climb a stile and turn left to reach a metalled road. Turn right here and follow the road back to the car park at the village hall.

*Black-and-white architecture in Staunton*

## ✚ To lengthen

Keep ahead at Waypoint 6, turn left on Scar Lane, then left again on a bridleway which peters out just short of the river, with its view of Brobury Scar. Return to Waypoint 6 to continue the main walk. This adds 1.6km (25min).

## Monnington's treasures

Monnington is a remarkably interesting little village, with Monnington Walk, St Mary's Church and a medieval big house, Monnington Court, which was begun in the 14th century and enlarged 300 years later.

Monnington Walk, a mile-long avenue alternating between yews and pines, was planted by Monnington Court's owner James Tomkins in 1623 to mark his election as an MP. A staunch Royalist, he was executed by the Parliamentarians in the English Civil War. The church, remodelled by his grandson Uvedall Tomkins in 1679, is an incredible time capsule, still lit by oil lamps and with original pews and furnishings.

*Looking back along the bridleway from Dolfach to Crafta Webb*

# WALK 9
## Merbach Hill from Bredwardine

| | |
|---|---|
| **Start/finish** | *Red Lion, Bredwardine* |
| **Locate** | *///isolating.from.shine* |
| **Cafes/pubs** | *Pub in Bredwardine* |
| **Transport** | *No public transport* |
| **Parking** | *Roadside parking in village* |
| **Toilets** | *No public toilets on route* |

**Time** 2hr 45min
**Distance** 7.8km (4.8 miles)
**Climb** 240m

**Curious earthworks by the Wye and a steady climb past a deserted settlement to the viewpoint on Merbach Hill**

From Bredwardine, with its church, castle mound and medieval fishponds, the route gains height steadily through Finestreet and Crafta Webb, a former squatter settlement with an extraordinary history, to the modest height of Merbach Hill, a renowned viewpoint overlooking dramatic meanders of the River Wye. Easy walking on a bridleway and then the Wye Valley Walk leads to a steep final descent to the village.

*The meandering River Wye below Merbach Hill*

*The bridleway by Bredwardine churchyard*

**1** Take the road towards Bredwardine bridge, fork right onto Church Lane and take the bridleway running between the church and the community orchard. Go past the overgrown mound of a late medieval castle and

ⓘ *Herefordshire's cider apple and perry pear orchards provide fruit for an increasing number of artisanal producers.*

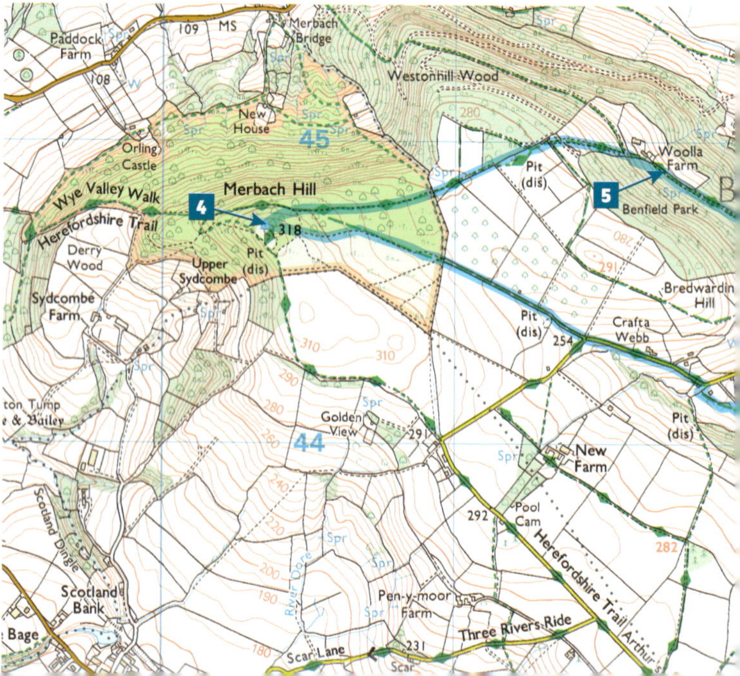

Pond Bay

some equally overgrown fishponds, then keep to the right of the much more substantial water feature of **Pond Bay**, another medieval fishpond. The ponds formed part of a medieval landscape which also included a kitchen garden, orchard and vineyard.

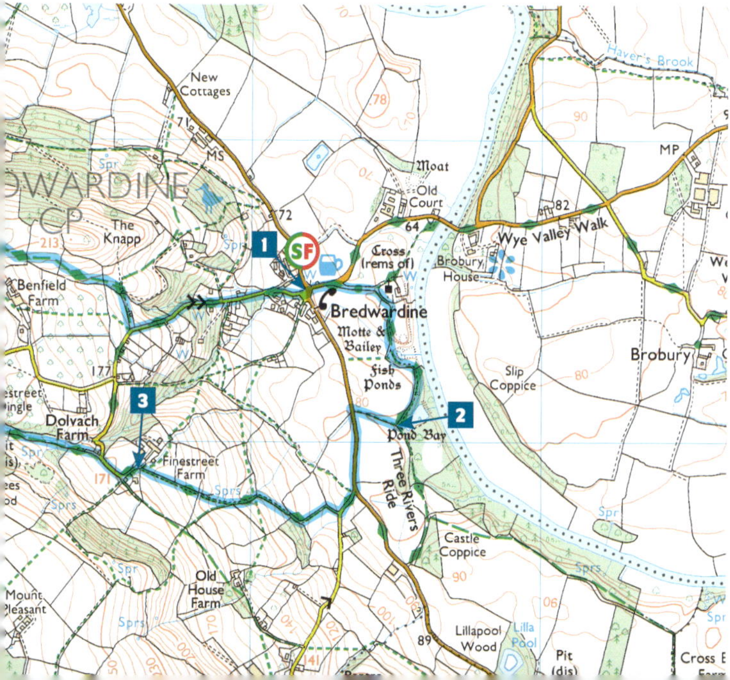

**2** Turn right over a stile and keep to the edge of the field to reach the B4352. Go briefly left along the mercifully quiet main road, turn right onto the Dorstone road and after 100m take the path on the right. It is vital to turn right at the top of the first field, to climb a grassy bank and reach a stile in

the left corner of the next field, then cross sheep pastures to reach **Finestreet Farm**. The farmhouse has some original 17th-century timber-framing.

**3** Use the farm's access road to reach the crumbling tarmac of Fine Street, then fork left on a splendid bridleway which runs alongside a deeply incised stream to reach a track. Turn right, then left on a metalled lane through the abandoned hamlet of **Crafta Webb**.

Crafta Webb was a squatter settlement established in the early 19th century following a bequest from a former tramp who became wealthy after emigrating to America. The settlement boasted its own grocer, tailor and shoemaker but by the 1920s was virtually deserted.

The lane climbs steadily, then bends sharply left; leave it here to take the bridleway straight ahead, which reaches the common land of **Merbach Hill**, taking a winding course to the bright white trig pillar marking the summit of the hill.

**4** Take the clear path going east, dropping down through woodland and then winding through bracken and rosebay willowherb in summer to reach the edge of the common. The

*View north from the summit of Merbach Hill*

way, now following the Wye Valley Walk, lies through a series of fields, then with woodland on either side as it approaches **Woolla Farm**. Bypass the farm to the right on a permissive path.

> The common land of Merbach Hill is noted for skylarks and birds of prey, and offers sensational views down to the impressive meanders of the River Wye and to hills in all directions, from the Malverns to Clee Hill, the Radnor Hills and the Black Mountains.

**5** Beyond the farm the stony track used by the Wye Valley Walk cuts through the woodland of **Benfield Park**, climbing past a viewpoint and then dropping down by a stream and swinging right down a track to meet a metalled road. Turn left and follow the road which descends steeply to **Bredwardine** before levelling out just before the Red Lion.

### ▬ To shorten

Take the direct path south-west from the start (ignoring paths left and right) to reach Finestreet Farm (Waypoint 3), omitting the earthworks south of Bredwardine church and saving 1.1km (20min).

*Autumn colours in Ferney Ground Covert*

# WALK 10
## Brilley and Whitney Court

**Time** 2hr
**Distance** 5.9km
(3.7 miles)
**Climb** 145m

**Excellent paths, wide views across the Wye valley and a fine nature reserve**

| | |
|---|---|
| **Start/finish** | *Brilley church* |
| **Locate** | *///expert.shape.amphibian* |
| **Cafes/pubs** | *None on route* |
| **Transport** | *No public transport* |
| **Parking** | *Small car park by church (HR3 6JF)* |
| **Toilets** | *No public toilets on route* |

Taking the Herefordshire Trail from Brilley church, this outstanding route uses a succession of well-marked woodland paths to reach the parkland of the Whitney Court estate, with extensive views across the Wye valley. It then cuts through the Brilley Dingle Nature Reserve and climbs an ancient sunken lane to return to Brilley.

*Looking across the Wye valley from Ferney Ground Covert*

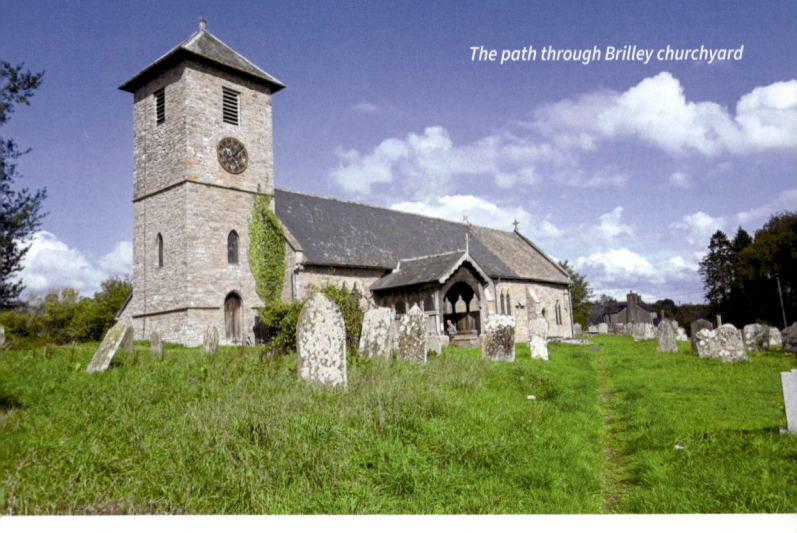

*The path through Brilley churchyard*

**1** Leave **Brilley** churchyard through a gate into a large field and follow the distinct path, aiming for a gate on the far side. The church tower with its wooden pyramid roof was rebuilt in 1912 after a fire destroyed its medieval predecessor. Skirt farm buildings, cross a drive and turn left onto a path (signposted as the Herefordshire Trail) which improves as it descends through a thin belt of woodland. Cross a little stream on a footbridge with a ford alongside, then turn left onto a gravelly track which climbs gently to reach a road.

**2** Go straight across the road, pass The Arbour and Montpellier Cottage and enter woodland, veering left when the Herefordshire Trail turns right. Climb through conifers to a gate, keep straight ahead on a narrow path and swing left at the edge of **Ferney Ground Covert**, now with the scarp face of the Black Mountains ahead. The path is well signposted as it curves through the wood, eventually emerging at a gate. Go diagonally across the field here to reach a lane.

**3** Walk down the lane past The Grange Farm and the entrance to **Whitney Court**, with its striking black-and-white stable block opposite.

A monument to Edwardian self-confidence, the striking neo-Tudor Whitney Court stands high above the Wye valley. When it was built the house had state-of-the-art central heating and one of the first private power plants in England.

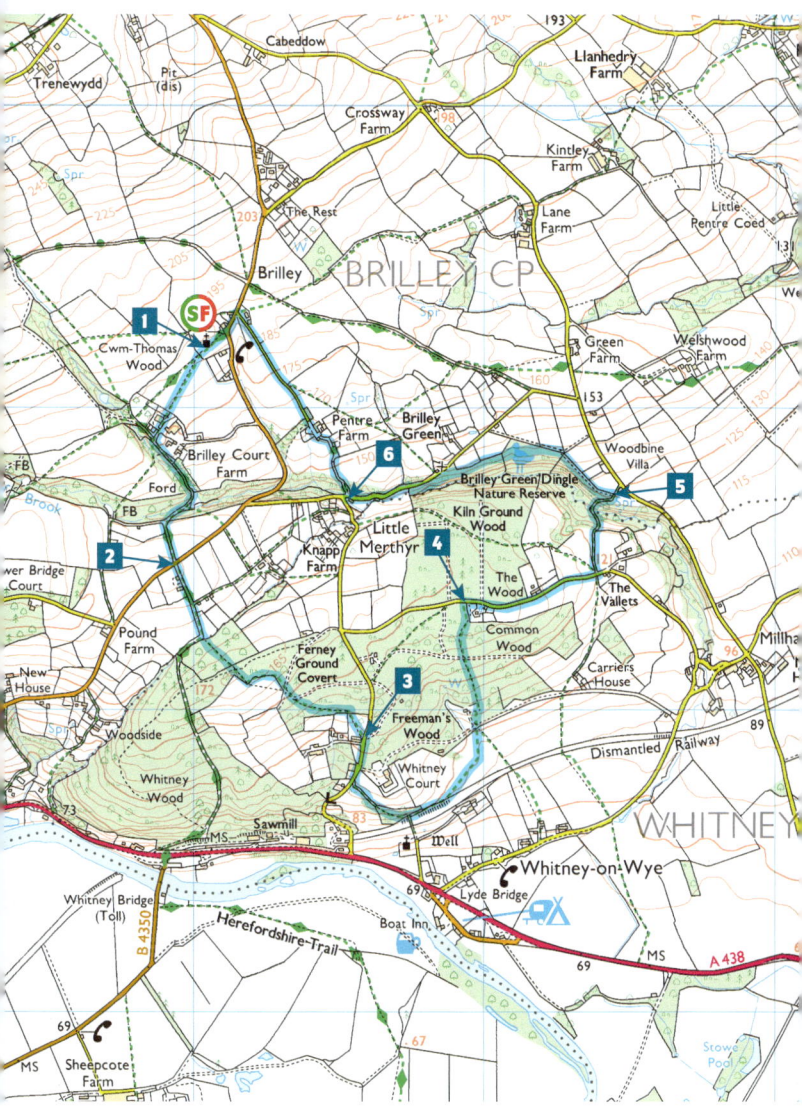

Take the path on the left, confined between tall hedges and a barbed wire fence, with the ground beyond falling away steeply towards the river. Carry straight on at a gate, the path now running alongside an abandoned railway line. A short diversion across the railway cutting leads to the attractive church at Whitney-on-Wye. Go through another gate and cut across parkland, now with Whitney Court prominent to the left, to pass through two kissing gates and take an excellent and almost straight path through **Common Wood** as far as a country lane.

**4** Turn right and follow the lane past **The Wood**, with Merbach Hill and the Burton Hills prominent beyond the neat fields of the Wye valley, and turn left at The Vallets onto a good path between trees. The lane becomes sunken and rutted as it descends to cross the Millhalf Brook on rough stepping stones and then climbs steadily. As the slope eases, turn sharp left to reach an information board at the entrance to **Brilley Green Dingle Nature Reserve**.

**The woodland nature reserve at Brilley Green Dingle, managed by the Herefordshire Wildlife Trust, supports a rich variety of plants and birds such as pied flycatchers. The Millhalf Brook is home to the threatened white-clawed crayfish, the UK's only native freshwater crayfish.**

*Whitney Court*

*The chapel in Brilley Green Dingle*

**5** Keep to the higher path through the nature reserve; it is narrow in places and can become overgrown in summer. The path twists and turns, crossing a surprisingly deep ravine on a footbridge. A galleried Calvinistic Methodist chapel dating from 1828 lies a few metres to the right of the path. Follow the path alongside the stream, with its rock steps, to an entrance to the reserve, and turn left along the lane towards a junction by a cottage.

**6** Turn right just before the junction onto a rocky track which becomes a sunken holloway with a little cliff to the right. When the slope eases the way forward becomes a green lane, swinging past **Pentre Farm** and the Old Rickyard onto a tarmac lane which reaches the road through Brilley by the Old Forge. The churchyard is 50m to the left.

*Looking south along the path from Cae-Higgin*

# WALK 11
## Rhydspence and Red Lane

**Time** 3hr
**Distance** 10.4km (6.5 miles)
**Climb** 280m

A varied walk on quiet lanes, drove roads and Offa's Dyke Path in the Radnorshire Hills

| | |
|---|---|
| **Start/finish** | Rhydspence Inn |
| **Locate** | ///brotherly.donates.contained |
| **Cafes/pubs** | Pub in Rhydspence |
| **Transport** | No public transport |
| **Parking** | Roadside parking opposite inn (HR3 6EU) |
| **Toilets** | No public toilets on route |

This is an enjoyable and very varied walk in the hills to the north of the Wye valley, using quiet country lanes, a superb green lane that was formerly a key route for drovers, and part of the Offa's Dyke Path long-distance trail. Historic sites include Bettws chapel, where the diarist Francis Kilvert preached, and the late medieval Rhydspence Inn.

*The medieval Rhydspence Inn*

**1** Leave Rhydspence by taking the country lane signposted to Brynafal, climbing steeply at first past Brynafal Cottage, **Bank of Pleasure** and the attractive group of buildings at **Bridge Court**. Keep straight on for 700m, then turn right at a T-junction, climbing past verges managed for wildlife, until the lane bends sharply to the right. The OS map shows footpaths offering a promising shortcut, but these are poorly signposted and difficult to follow.

**2** Turn left along Red Lane, initially a stony track heading west, with the Wye valley below to the left, then fork right at a junction of tracks, going through a gate to follow a green track across the common land of **Milton Hill**. Red Lane was an important drove road by the 18th century, when 30,000 Welsh black cattle were sent through Hereford each year. Beyond a second gate the green lane, often deeply rutted, is more constricted, but its wide

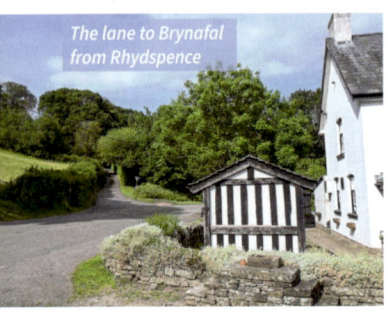

The lane to Brynafal from Rhydspence

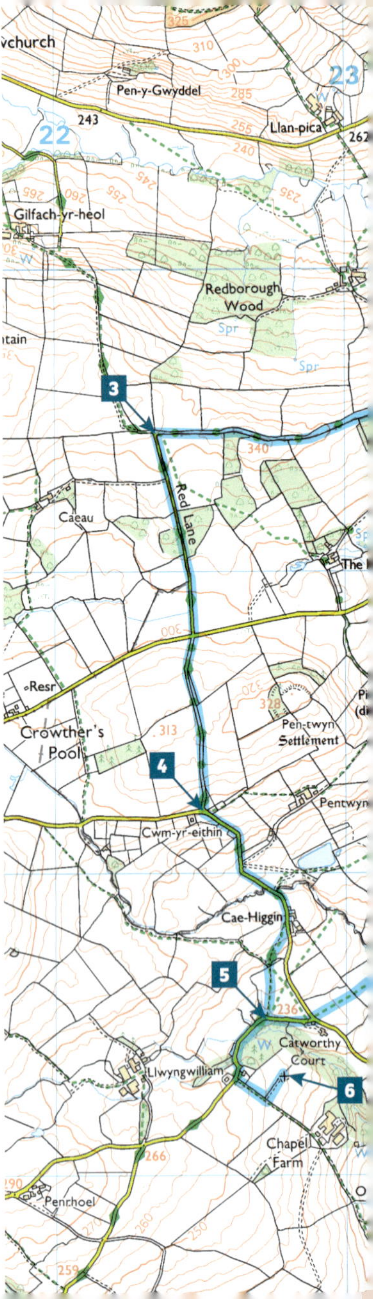

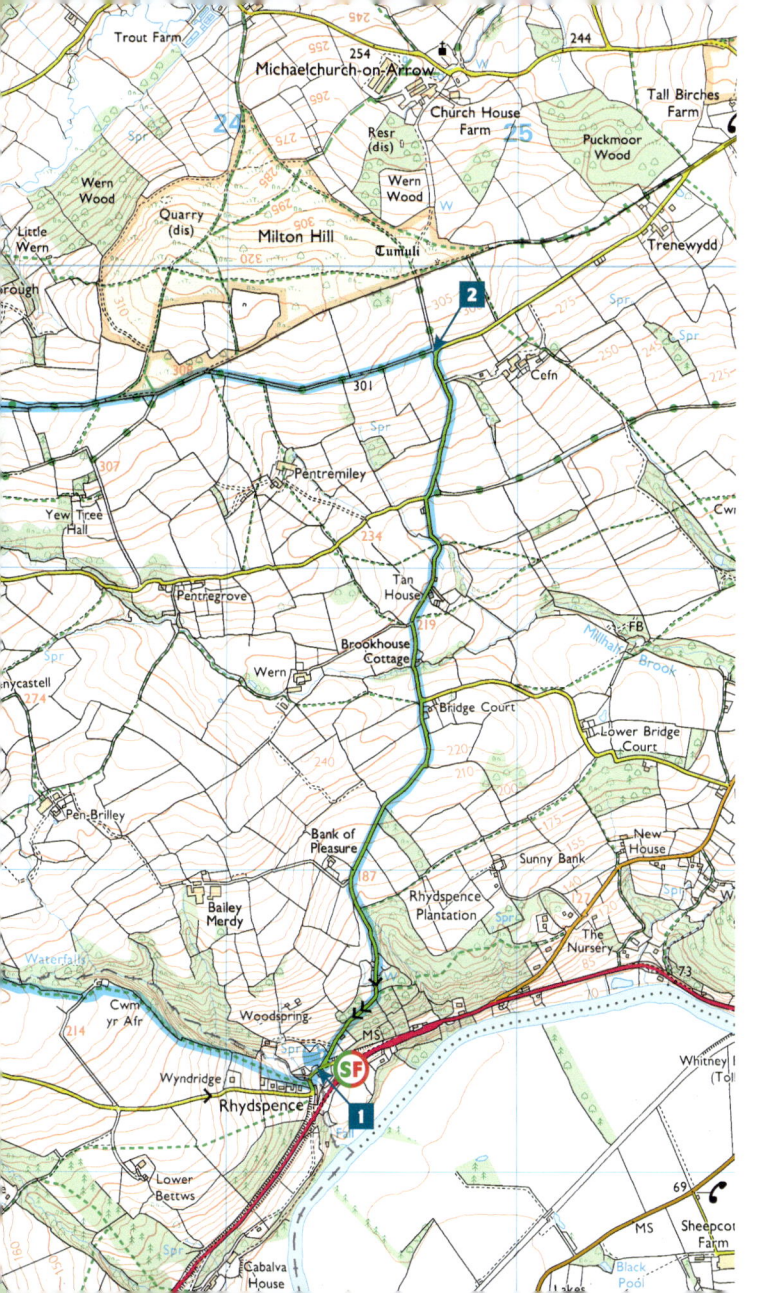

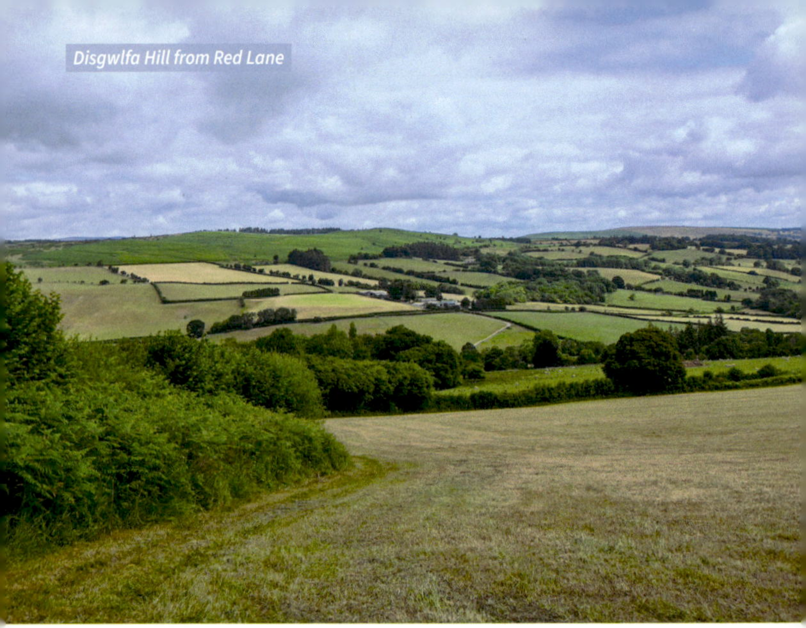

Disgwlfa Hill from Red Lane

verges confirm its status as a former drove road. There are glimpses of Disgwlfa Hill across the Arrow valley before the lane reaches Offa's Dyke Path.

**3** Turn left here to follow the long-distance path (still named as **Red Lane**), at first a gravelly track but soon a roughly surfaced lane. Go straight across at a crossroads, now on turf again, climbing the wide drove road with a collapsing stone wall to the right. The way lies through sheep pastures until the track narrows after a final gate, reaching a country lane at **Cwm-yr-eithin**.

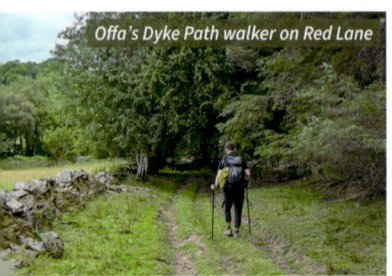

Offa's Dyke Path walker on Red Lane

**4** Turn left along the road and follow its twisting course as it dips down to cross a stream, then turn right through an oversized kissing gate opposite **Cae-Higgin** onto a splendid green path which clearly indicates the route through two fields to a gate giving access onto a minor road.

**5** Turn right, following the road through woodland and over a stream as far as Chapel House. Now turn immediately left (unsignposted) onto a tarmac lane descending scenically towards the Wye valley. A gate on the left gives access to the isolated **Bettws chapel**.

Bettws chapel-of-ease occupies a stunning site high above the valley. When the diarist Francis Kilvert, curate of Clyro, visited in February 1870 his beard froze to his mackintosh and he had to break the ice in the font to perform a baptism.

**6** Retrace your steps to Waypoint 5 and carry on along the lane to a junction. Go straight ahead into a field, crossing this to a gate, before swinging to the right across a second field, making for a stile in the far corner. Keep to the left-hand edge of a big field, locate a dilapidated stile hidden in the far corner and cross the lane leading to **Cwm yr Afr** cottage. Climb another stile and keep ahead, the path faint but the direction obvious. Cross a final field, with bungalows to the right, to reach the road by the Rhydspence Inn.

A classic example of a drovers' inn, the black-and-white Rhydspence Inn dates from 1380. By the 17th century it had become a focal point for drovers on the Black Ox trail from the Welsh uplands to markets in Gloucester, Oxford and London.

**— To shorten**

Turn left at Waypoint 5 and omit the visit to Bettws chapel, saving 1km (20min).

## Offa's Dyke Path

A spectacular 285km (177 mile) route from Chepstow on the Severn estuary to Prestatyn in north Wales, Offa's Dyke Path criss-crosses the England–Wales border. For around a third of its length it closely follows the remarkable 8th-century earthwork built by the Mercian King Offa – the longest linear earthwork in Britain, and a statement of political control in the Welsh borders. The path crosses the River Wye at Hay, then climbs up to join the Red Lane drove route before heading north towards Newchurch and Kington.

*Track climbing out of Cusop Dingle by the Old Mill*

# WALK 12
## Cusop Hill

**Time** 2hr 15min
**Distance** 6.4km (4 miles)
**Climb** 250m

| | |
|---|---|
| **Start/finish** | Lychgate at Cusop churchyard |
| **Locate** | ///trailing.obstinate.volcano |
| **Cafes/pubs** | None on route |
| **Transport** | No public transport |
| **Parking** | Small car park by church, donation requested (HR3 5RF) |
| **Toilets** | No public toilets on route |

**A remarkable churchyard, an exhilarating climb to a quiet summit with an all-round panorama, and an attractive valley**

Cusop is very close to Hay-on-Wye but seems a world away from the bustling book town. The churchyard is full of surprises, and this walk is well signposted and generally easy, though with a sustained climb to reach the summit slopes of Cusop Hill. There is an attractive descent into Cusop Dingle, once a hive of industry but now a quiet hamlet alongside a rippling brook.

*Woodland track near Craigau*

*The lychgate at the start of the walk*

**1** From the lychgate walk through the churchyard, passing ancient yew trees, to find a gate into a field. Turn right along the field boundary, find a gate in the field corner and gain height crossing a second enormous field, with the isolated house at **Capodolwyn** prominent on the steep slopes ahead. Keep left of a lone oak tree to clamber up to a somewhat rustic stile.

**2** Go straight ahead over the stile, cutting through bracken to a waymark post. Turn right here and climb on a narrow path, eventually picking up a green track which leads to a little quarry. The way ahead is obvious across a large field, with the hillside dropping away to the right and views of Hay Bluff and the Black Mountain scarp opening up ahead. Swing left to a stile and head diagonally across a second field with the summit of **Cusop Hill** to the right. Cusop Hill is a sprawling expanse of flat-topped moorland with wonderful views eastwards across much of Herefordshire, and westwards into the Black Mountains. Go to the right of a lone tree before cutting across towards a stand of fir trees to find a gate onto a country lane by **Pen-shinkle**.

*The northern ridge of the Black Mountains seen from Cusop Hill*

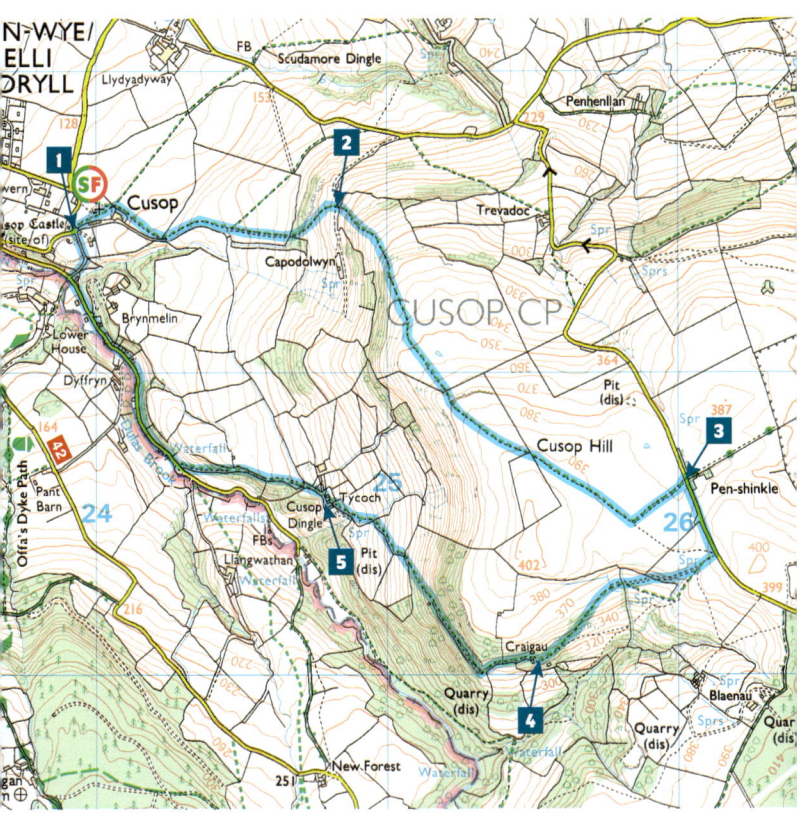

**3** Turn right along the road for 250m, then climb a stile and head to the left of a group of trees to pick up a faint track, but as soon as the ground levels out cross the stream and climb up to reach a field gate. Go straight ahead along a good green track which drops down into woodland to reach the deserted buildings at **Craigau**.

**4** Turn up to the right immediately before the ruins (the path may be obstructed by bracken in summer, in which case climb the hillside just beyond the ruins). The objective is a stile which gives access to a delightful path with a fence and later an old hedgerow to the left. The route then descends an open, bracken-covered

An unexpected resident in Cusop Dingle

(i) *Described by former US president Bill Clinton as 'the Woodstock of the mind', the book festival in Hay-on-Wye takes place in late May and early June.*

slope and crosses two meadows to arrive at **Tycoch** Farm.

**5** Take the narrow lane leading from the farm to the road through **Cusop Dingle**, with **Dulas Brook** – the boundary between England and Wales – running to the left of the road. Cusop Dingle was once home to five mills, quarries, limekilns and a cider house. The way lies past Paper Mill Cottage, which hints at the industrial past of the valley. Turn right at the Old Mill, now on a little track through woodland, to pass the scanty remains of **Cusop Castle** and arrive back at the churchyard.

## Cusop churchyard

The churchyard is full of interest, with enormous yew trees up to 2000 years old and the graves of Richard Booth, who reinvented Hay-on-Wye as a book town, William Seward and Kitty Armstrong. Seward was a travelling preacher who was attacked by a mob while preaching in Hay in 1740 and died a week later, becoming the first Methodist martyr. Kitty Armstrong was the wife and, in 1921, the victim of the notorious Hay Poisoner, Herbert Rowse Armstrong, the only English solicitor ever to have been hanged for murder.

# WALK 13
## The Begwns

**Time** 2hr 30min
**Distance** 7.2km
(4.5 miles)
**Climb** 145m

| | |
|---|---|
| **Start/finish** | *North-east corner of common, above Crossvilog Farm* |
| **Locate** | *///humans.giraffes.sleepy* |
| **Cafes/pubs** | *None on route* |
| **Transport** | *No public transport* |
| **Parking** | *Layby with a few spaces at start (LD2 3JW)* |
| **Toilets** | *No public toilets on route* |

**A wonderful moorland common with spectacular mountain views and a huge network of wide green tracks**

High above the Wye valley at Clyro, the Begwns is an outstanding resource for walkers, a big common cared for by the National Trust and criss-crossed by a myriad of broad green tracks which provide easy walking on gentle slopes. The highest point, The Roundabout, has a stand of commemorative trees enclosed by a stone wall, while the Monk's Pond is a tranquil oasis for ducks and grebes.

*The final stage above Crossvilog*

**1** Take the track going sharply left through bracken to reach a narrow metalled lane on the southern edge of the common. Turn right here and follow the lane until it swings left towards **Llowes Hall**. The former name of Llowes Hall was Tir-y-Beddau, suggesting the presence of graves in the area, perhaps the result of a battle. Leave the lane to the right here on a wide green track. The track passes close to the deserted ruins of **Bird's Nest** Farm, just to the left in the bracken.

**2** A gate on the left gives a view of **Gogia** Farm and the path then descends to cross a damp area. Swing left, following the wall denoting the boundary of the common, with the Monk's Pond clearly in view ahead. Keep to the left of the pond, pass a

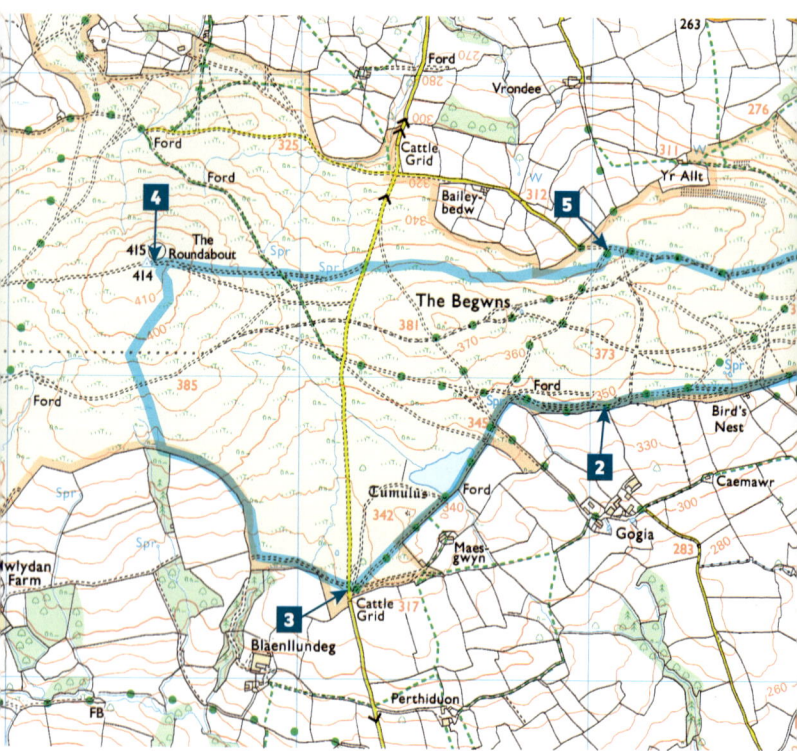

Approaching the Monk's Pond

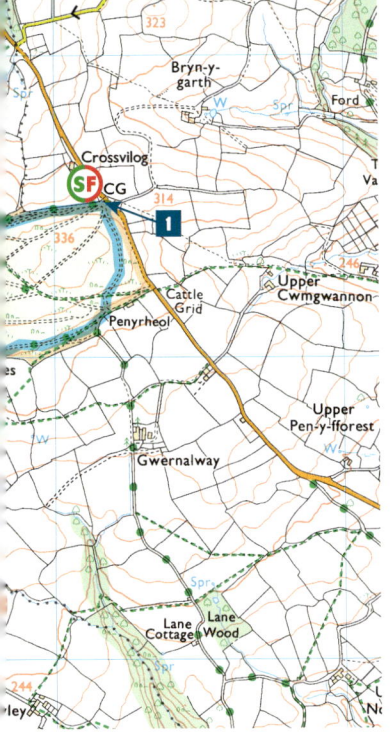

Bronze Age tumulus, and reach a narrow country road just by a **cattle grid**.

**Deceptively natural in appearance, the Monk's Pond was actually constructed in the 1960s to control the water supply to Gogia Farm. The lake is a haven for wildlife, with Canada geese, great crested grebe, mallards and coot all resident here.**

**3** Go slightly right across the road, ford two small streams, swing right again and then climb steadily, with the edge of the common to the left – the path is not on the OS map but is clear on the ground. A long narrow strip of woodland comes up to meet the common; veer right here to climb up towards **The Roundabout**, passing through gorse and rough grassland. A final stretch on a narrow path through bracken leads to the white trig pillar marking the summit of the hill.

*The Roundabout from above the Monk's Pond*

**Trees were planted at The Roundabout on the summit of the Begwns in 1887, to commemorate the golden jubilee of Queen Victoria. The stone wall enclosing the little wood was substantially restored in 2000 to mark the millennium.**

*Yellowhammer on the Begwns*

**4** Walk around The Roundabout and then take the obvious broad green path, descending to cross the narrow metalled road again. Take the path heading slightly left and slightly uphill, with the ruins of the former **Bailey-bedw** Farm down to the left. The path rises to pass a ring cairn on a little hill; take the middle of three paths here to ford a stream by a little pond. The long whale-back ridge of Llanbedr Hill is very prominent beyond the village of Painscastle.

**5** Continue eastwards on closely cropped turf, dropping down to the edge of the common above **Crossvilog** Farm. Yellowhammer and stonechat can often be seen – and heard – in this area. Follow the fence along the edge of the common back to the little parking area.

*The summit ridge of the Begwns*

## The Begwns

The extensive upland common of the Begwns, largely bracken-covered but with areas of grassland, heather and gorse, was given to the National Trust in 1992. It supports a range of heathland butterflies, dragonflies and brown hares, together with birds such as buzzards and red kites. In summer lapwing, curlew and golden plover breed here.

The common is full of historical interest too, with burial cairns and, on the western slopes, the deserted medieval village of Pentre Jack, its house platforms and trackways still traceable.

*The extraordinary interior of Llanelieu church*

# WALK 14
## Common Bychan and Rhos Fawr

**Time** 3hr
**Distance** 8.8km (5.5 miles)
**Climb** 270m

**Quiet lanes and superb green tracks across upland commons in the shadow of the Black Mountains**

| | |
|---|---|
| **Start/finish** | *Nant-y-Gollen, south of Felindre* |
| **Locate** | *///departure.boggles.gobbling* |
| **Cafes/pubs** | *None on route* |
| **Transport** | *No public transport* |
| **Parking** | *Limited roadside parking near start* |
| **Toilets** | *No public toilets on route* |

This is a wonderful walk in the Black Mountain foothills, crossing three upland commons with abundant birdlife, including yellowhammers and stonechats. Wild ponies roam Rhos Fawr, the largest common, while the church at Llanelieu is fascinating, with a highly unusual medieval rood screen. The return to the little village of Felindre is intricate but well signposted, and includes sheep pastures, open woodland and buttercup meadows.

*Ponies grazing on Rhos Fawr Common*

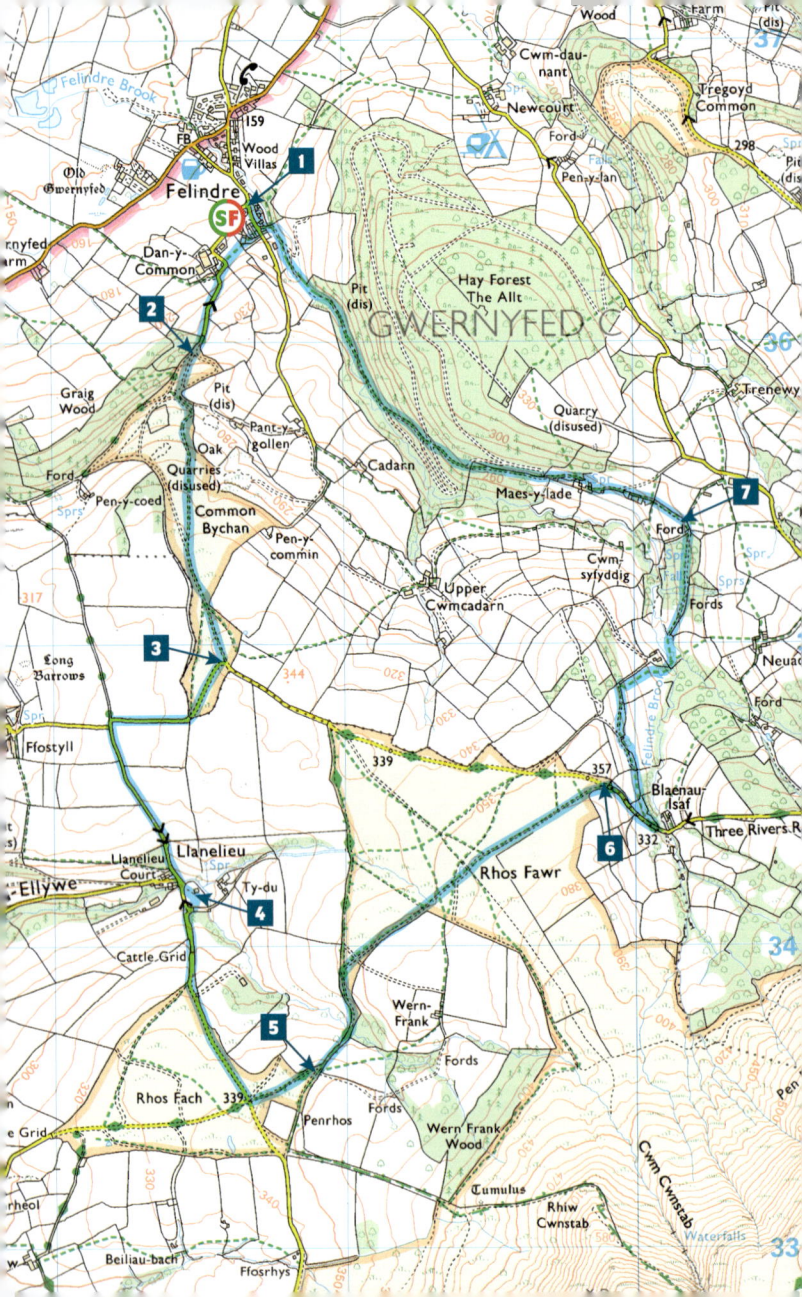

**1** Take the minor road towards Pant-y-Gollen but quickly go up steps onto a path which crosses a field to reach a gated lane running above **Dan-y-Common** Farm. Go through a gate into Bannau Brycheiniog National Park to find a footpath rising to the left.

**2** Climb the footpath, making steady progress through the bracken on springy green turf. Turn briefly left at a crossroad of paths, then turn right to continue across the higher slopes of **Common Bychan**, with the ridge of the Black Mountains an increasingly prominent feature to the left. The green track widens as it traverses gentle slopes, swinging slightly left to meet an unfenced and very narrow road.

Common Bychan is one of a number of small remnants of common land on the hillslopes between

ⓘ *The Black Mountains, the eastern range in Bannau Brycheiniog, rise 600m above the Wye valley around Hay-on-Wye.*

the escarpment of the Black Mountains and the lower, more productive farmland.

**3** Turn right along the road, go through a gate and after a long straight stretch turn left at a minor crossroads. The lane now dips down increasingly steeply into the hidden hamlet of **Llanelieu**, passing the 17th-century Court and crossing a stream. Climb steps on the left to enter the churchyard.

Cared for by the Friends of Friendless Churches, Llanelieu is delightfully situated and full

*The path through Llanelieu churchyard*

of interest inside, with a highly unusual red-painted 14th-century rood screen and a collection of wall paintings.

**4** Leave at the top of the churchyard, climb steeply up the lane and then walk on grass alongside the road across **Rhos Fach** Common. Turn left at a crossroads onto a gravelly track, signposted as the Three Rivers Ride, and keep on the track towards Wern-Frank until a signpost indicates a left turn just before a gate.

**5** Take the track on the left, cross a stream and climb a rocky path, emerging onto a plateau overlooking the distant Wye valley. Keep right on the plateau, following the post-and-wire fence on the edge of **Rhos Fawr** and when the fence ends keep to the same direction, the grassy path clearly seen cutting through bracken and gorse. Keep ahead to reach a narrow mountain road close to a gate.

**6** Go through the gate and down the road, then turn left over a stile onto a footpath just before **Blaenau-Isaf**. A gap in the hedge leads into a second field, with a left fork into a third; follow the right-hand boundary to find a holloway and a helpful waymark post. Walk to the right of a field barn, then keep an old hedgerow on the right to find a stile. Turn sharp right here and descend past buildings on a very

*Crossing Rhos Fawr, with Twmpa (Lord Hereford's Knob) beyond*

*Looking down the Felindre Brook valley*

well-signposted route across fords and through woodland. Leave the trees and cross a field to a stile giving access to a grassy track.

**7** Ignore the track and instead turn left, crossing a field to an obvious stile. Pass farm buildings and cross the access track to the **Maes-y-lade** activity centre, looking for a blue bridleway sign on a gate. The bridleway is easy to follow, though muddy in a few places, then becomes stony as it crosses a forest road. Meet a second gravelly forest road and turn right, heading directly back to the start of the walk.

## – To shorten

Turn left at Waypoint 3 and walk alongside the country lane to Waypoint 6, saving 2km (35min) but missing Llanelieu church and the glorious expanse of Rhos Fawr Common.

*ⓘ The upland commons above Hay-on-Wye are home to breeding meadow pipits, wheatears, stonechats and yellowhammers, with buzzards and red kites in the skies above.*

*The dry bed of Brechfa Pool after a period of drought*

# WALK 15
## Brechfa Pool

**Time** 2hr 45min
**Distance** 8.5km
(5.3 miles)
**Climb** 220m

A delightful
upland lake and
easy walking on
open common
land with
extraordinary
mountain views

| | |
|---|---|
| **Start/finish** | *Phone box by Brechfa Pool* |
| **Locate** | *///crawling.whistle.drifters* |
| **Cafes/pubs** | *None on route* |
| **Transport** | *No public transport* |
| **Parking** | *Informal parking by Brechfa Pool (LD3 0NW)* |
| **Toilets** | *No public toilets on route* |

The open moorland of Brechfa Common provides easy walking on wide green tracks through bracken, with an astonishing backdrop of the three mountain ranges in Bannau Brycheiniog National Park (the Black Mountains, the Brecon Beacons and the Carmarthen Fan). Brechfa Pool, with its rare plants and array of breeding birds, together with waders on spring and autumn migration, is a peaceful oasis high above the Wye valley.

*The western slopes of Mynydd Forest near Nant-yr-Arian*

**1** Walk north along the lane from the phone box, away from the pool. *The building near the phone box is the Calvinistic Methodist Bethesda chapel, founded in 1791.* On reaching the common take a good path on the right through bracken, merging onto a wider track and passing **Whitehall** Farm and a seasonal pond, with dramatic views of the soaring peaks of Bannau Brycheiniog behind. Just after a lone holly tree, turn left into a narrow drove between fences. Keep straight on to reach a minor road.

**2** Turn left along the road, then quickly right at a waymark post just before the Wernished Farm access track. The route now follows the bridleway as it gradually gains height across **Brechfa Common**. The track initially hugs the left-hand edge of the

*The start of the walk*

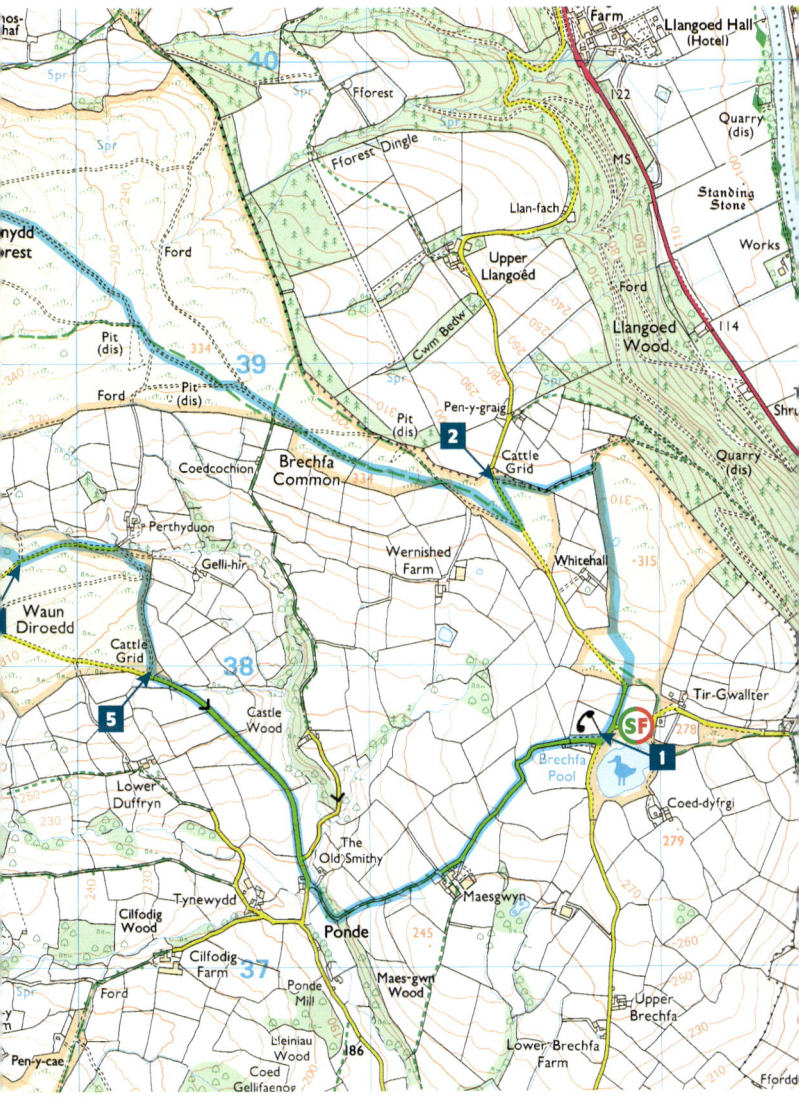

common, cutting through bracken and passing above Coedcochion Farm before curving up the higher slopes of **Mynydd Forest** on a good surface of springy turf, with meadow pipits and skylarks for company as the trig point is reached.

Mynydd Forest is an unremarkable summit, only 400m high, but it boasts a remarkable panorama, including the Carmarthen Fan, Pen-y-Fan and Cribyn, the Black Mountains, the Herefordshire hills, the Begwns and Llanbedr Hill.

**3** Take the left-hand of two paths from the trig point on Mynydd Forest, descending gently across the open common until, just beyond **Nant-yr-arian,** turning left onto a path which skirts the enclosed fields by the farm and reaches the edge of the common. Turn right here, with bracken to the right and a tall hedge to the left, and when the hedgerow ends pick up a track winding through rough grass to reach a gravelly track and, just to the right, the narrow road leading to Perthyduon.

*The track across the common at Waun Diroedd*

*Brechfa Pool*

**4** Head left along the road towards **Perthyduon**, but leave this to the right on a rough track when the road swings left. After only a few metres, take the good track on the right, and then fork left onto a green trod that snakes through the bracken of **Waun Diroedd**, hugging the eastern boundary of the common. After crossing a marshy area the route becomes a clear track and reaches a road at a cattle grid.

**5** Turn left and follow the road for some 800m into the hamlet of **Ponde**. Shortly after a lane comes in from the left by the Old Smithy, look for a little green lane on the left when the road veers right. The lane is narrow and can be marshy at first, but soon improves.

After only 150m turn left again, this time on a rocky track initially accompanied by a stream as far as the big farm complex at **Maesgwyn**. Carry on along a narrow tarmac lane to return to **Brechfa Pool**.

Brechfa Pool is a small, shallow lake, which can disappear completely after long dry periods. Home to rare plants, including pennyroyal, orange foxtail grass and the endangered pillwort, it hosts breeding lapwing and reed bunting, with curlew on the common.

*The site of Wilton quay from Wilton bridge (Walk 2)*

© Mike Dunn 2026
First edition 2026
ISBN: 978 1 78631 289 1
eISBN: 978 1 78765 256 9

Printed in China on responsibly sourced paper on behalf of Latitude Press Ltd.
A catalogue record for this book is available from the British Library.
All photographs are by Chris and Mike Dunn.
Cover illustration of Ross-on-Wye by Clare Crooke.

© Crown copyright and database rights 2026 OS AC0000810376

Cicerone's EU representative for GPSR compliance is Easy Access System Europe, Mustamäe tee 50, 10621 Tallinn, Estonia. Email gpsr.requests@easproject.com.

# CICERONE

Cicerone Press, Juniper House, Murley Moss, Oxenholme Road,
Kendal, Cumbria, LA9 7RL

cicerone.co.uk

## Updates to this Guide

While every effort is made to ensure the accuracy of guidebooks as they go to print, changes can occur during the lifetime of an edition. Any updates that we know of for this guide will be on the Cicerone website (cicerone.co.uk/1289/updates), so please check before planning your trip. We also advise that you check information about transport, accommodation and shops locally. Even rights of way can be altered over time. We are always grateful for information about any discrepancies between a guidebook and the facts on the ground, sent by email to updates@cicerone.co.uk.

Register your book: To sign up to receive free updates, special offers and GPX files where available, create a Cicerone account and register your purchase via the 'My Account' tab at cicerone.co.uk.

# USEFUL INFORMATION

### Travel

Transport for Wales tfw.wales

Great Western Railway gwr.com

West Midlands Railway westmidlandsrailway.co.uk

CrossCountry crosscountrytrains.co.uk

Bus times bustimes.org

### Tourism and nature bodies

Wales Tourist Board visitwales.com

Visit Herefordshire visitherefordshire.co.uk

The National Trust nationaltrust.org.uk

RSPB rspb.org.uk

Herefordshire Wildlife Trust herefordshirewt.org

### Tourist information centres

Hay-on-Wye hay-on-wye.co.uk

Hereford tel 01432 383837

Ross-on-Wye tel 01989 562373